God doesn't play dice...
       ~Albert Einstein 1945

SURVIVING COINCIDENTAL HISTORY

JOHN J PATERSON

Copyright © 2025 JJ Paterson
All rights reserved.

Published by Hadal Publishing
66 Wood Street, White Gum Valley
Western Australia, 6162

A catalogue record for this
book is available from the
National Library of
Australia.

Author: Paterson, J.J.
Title: Surviving Coincidental History
ISBN: 978-0-646-71406-6
Subjects: Biography, Adventure, Travel, Discovery, Non-Fiction

Cover Artwork. Chris Bowman. Various sources.

The descriptions, the experiences and the words of this
story are the author's own.

All rights reserved. No part of this publication may be reproduced,
stored in a retrieval system or transmitted in any form or by any
means, electronic, mechanical, photocopying, recording or otherwise,
without prior written permission of the copyright holder.

The scanning, uploading, and distributing of this book via the Internet
or any other means without the publisher's permission is illegal and
punishable by law. Your support of the author's rights is appreciated.

DEDICATION

When life hangs by a thread and survival seems highly unlikely, we all need a friend like my old sailing mate, "Skipper" Robin Jeffries. However, the official report on the loss of 'Snizort' did not mention Robin, the true hero of the day. There should have been some acknowledgement that Robin so justly deserved. This was another reason that drove me to put pen to paper.

Thanks, Robin, for saving my life.
JJ.

PROLOGUE

The truth is this odd intergenerational saga began around 200 years ago. When I first started researching my family archives, I expected to uncover some surprises. I soon realised that I had become part of the same recurring historical twist of fate. So, after conducting extensive research to the best of my knowledge, the following three main stories are factually correct.

Headlines, *The Eastern Cape Herald*. Cape Town, South Africa,1880. 'The Steamship American has foundered en route to Cape Town off the coast of West Africa.'

On her passenger list is a prominent South African politician, John J Paterson, who is overdue for the opening of the Cape Town parliament.

1942. WW2 The SS CERINTHUS is torpedoed off the coast of West Africa. Several crew members survived the ordeal, including Second Engineer John J. Paterson, after whom I am named.

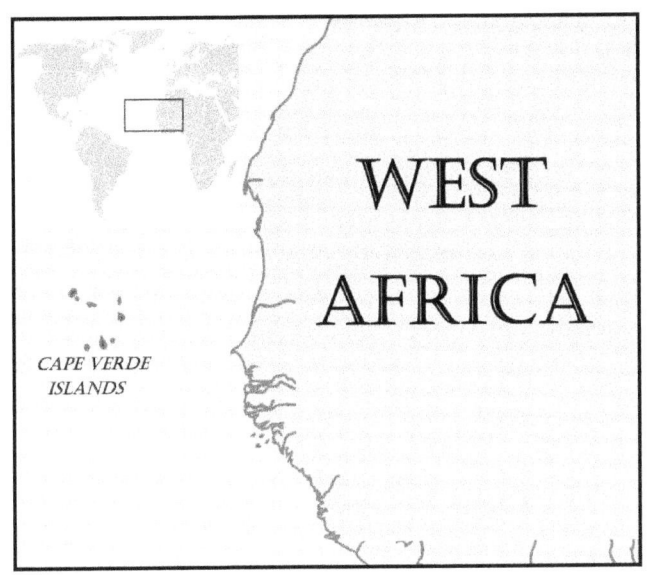

CAPE VERDE ISLANDS & WEST AFRICA

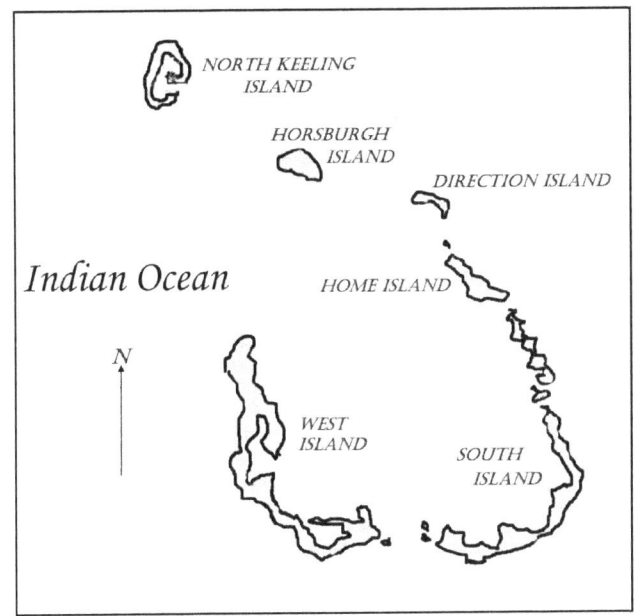

COCOS - KEELING ISLANDS

CHRISTMAS 1991

THE DELIVERY GAME

How it all started. A sailing pal, Robin Jeffries, a delivery skipper at the Fremantle Sailing Club, asked me if I could help him with a yacht delivery and, if things worked out, possibly start a marine delivery business together. Robin knew I was at a loose end, so yes, I was interested, but that casually made decision would set me on a life-changing course. Robin would be the skipper-navigator, while I would handle the deck work, the financials, and most of the cooking (not Robin's strong point).

LOTUS 2

A brief description of my introduction to the yacht delivery business follows. Our first job together was to take a 34-foot cruising yacht called Lotus 2 from the Fremantle Sailing Club down to Albany, a town on the southern coastline of Western Australia. The new yacht owner, a local Albany farmer with zero sailing skills, had recently bought the SS 34, a yacht with a good pedigree, and sailing would become his new hobby. He initially planned to make the voyage to Albany with Robin to get some hands-on experience. But as it was harvesting time, towards the end of the year, he had to take off at short notice back to the farm once the paperwork was done and his boat was good to go, leaving Robin with no crew.

That's when I came into the picture. Until then, all my former sailing had been done in local waters, racing with friends close inshore or on the Swan River. So, a 350 nautical mile offshore voyage around Cape Leeuwin, a headland on the southwestern corner of West Australia, where the Southern Ocean meets the Indian Ocean, sounded like a challenge, a new experience, and a bonus. I would be getting paid for doing what I did as a hobby—great! Robin had already made this trip a number of times, so I naively thought. What can go wrong? I was in safe hands. Robin and the farmer, whom I didn't meet until we sailed into Albany—and I still can't remember his name, had already prepared the boat for the voyage, so all I had to do was get my kit onboard and let a couple of my friends know that I would be disappearing for a week or so. Robin was keen to leave as soon as possible, as we only had a week left before Christmas.

I had heard tales around the club of some horrendous voyages around the Leeuwin, so out of curiosity, I did a little research and, to my surprise, discovered that Cape Leeuwin is rated as the fifth worst weather corner in the world. Hmm, something to think about.

A frantic day, all last-minute stuff, and we had Lotus 2 supplied with enough food and water for a week at sea, plus a bottle of rum and two cartons of beer; it was time to go. According to Robin, the weather patterns towards the end of the year are great for a run South, so with now only a week left before Christmas, Lotus 2 slipped out of Fremantle, a beautiful summer day, Robin at the helm and a fresh sea breeze to accompany us as we headed west out past Rottnest Island. Around fifteen miles off the coast, Robin spun the wheel for a new heading south to Albany, our next stop. Once we were well underway, Robin switched on the autopilot and pulled out a cardboard tube containing one of his marine charts. (Ocean navigation was a new learning curve for me) We carefully went through his planned route south together, keeping well offshore until we rounded the Cape Leeuwin lighthouse and then another 170 miles southeast along the southern coast to King George Sound and the town of Albany. If we can make 100 or so miles a day, we should easily reach Albany in 4 days and, with a bit of luck, still arrive home in time for Christmas. Once Robin was happy that I had a rough understanding of our planned route south, it was time for him to take a break and for me to have my first four-hour watch at the helm; we had left Fremantle shortly before lunch, so the coast had slipped over the horizon hours ago.

CAPE LEEUWIN

Before he disappeared below, Robin asked me to keep a sharp eye, as we would be close to the main shipping lanes. Then he headed off to his bunk. I took over the helm and disengaged the autopilot. I wanted to get a feel for the boat, and she felt great. For the next four hours, it was Lotus 2 and me gliding across the ocean swells together, and for a change, I felt the universe was smiling down on me, that lucky to be alive feeling. An hour before the end of my first watch, the sun's last dying glow slipped below the horizon, and night quickly set in. It's hard to describe the feeling I experienced that first night alone at the helm, with just the comforting dim red glow from the compass. Peaceful might do! And then Robin poked his head out of the companionway to check on me and the weather. "Hi, any probs?" me, "No, everything seems fine." Robin took the helm, and I headed below for a meal and then my bunk, unsure how I would sleep after my first full day at sea. I needn't have worried; I fell asleep instantly. As we ventured further south, the wind dropped to a zephyr. Lotus 2 slowed down, barely making a couple of knots. I woke up hours later to the sound of Robin starting our little two-cylinder diesel engine. He mentioned earlier that the farmer had refuelled the boat and told him we had a 200-mile cruising range. That sounded very economical, or so we thought!

For the next couple of days, we mainly needed to keep the engine running in fluky wind conditions, so we motor-sailed on and off to within 15 miles north of the Cape Leeuwin lighthouse. Robin was warning me we had to be wary of shipping close to this corner of the world when, suddenly, our engine sputtered out, and try as we might, that engine would not start again. We had only logged a little over 100 engine miles, so we shouldn't have run out of fuel, but that's what it sounded like, and the fuel gauge was stuck. Robin was concerned that we would flatten our batteries if we kept hitting the starter motor. So, with hardly a breeze, we were moving, but only just.

SEA FOG

Late afternoon, we were trying to bleed the injectors. I was hand-cranking the engine when we could see the fingers of a sea fog approaching, slowly creeping over the boat. Within 10 minutes, our visibility dropped to near zero, and a white blanket enveloped Lotus 2, something I had never encountered before. Eerie is definitely the word. We were ghosting along on a smooth, rolling sea of white with no engine, close to a main shipping lane and just a few miles off a dangerous headland. Robin didn't show any concern; he reckoned that capital ships stay well off the coast when rounding the Leeuwin, and the sea fog would only last a short while. It's a common occurrence in these parts where the two oceans meet due to the temperature difference, and any capital ship rounding the Cape in sea fog would sound their fog horns. I thought that all sounded logical but not very reassuring. We weren't really moving, and we couldn't see a thing! This wasn't a good situation. Then, there was this unnerving silence while the sea fog seemed to press down around us and the boat. According to Robin's calculations, I knew we were still around 15 miles or more northwest of the Cape, but I still couldn't help but try to listen out for the sound of waves breaking on rocks. When we heard an almighty roar, followed by a deafening crash, I was startled. We both froze, listening, straining to hear something, but that was it; nothing, no other sound, and we still had no visibility. The fog, the night, and the silence closed in around us again. I said, "What the hell was that? It sounded so close." Robin reckoned he had never experienced anything like that in his life, but "You know what, JJ, I think maybe that was a whale breaching, and it was bloody close." The sea fog persisted until close to midnight. As it cleared, it was reassuring to see the flash from the Leeuwin Light. Robin took over the helm, but there was hardly enough wind to keep us on course—time to hit my bunk after a nervous night. Robin woke me four hours later with a hot coffee. "Morning, JJ, still bugger all wind, mate." We lost most of the next day like that, just moving before a breeze picked up, and then it was a cold southerly right on the nose. We had to bash south into it for the rest of the day and finally cleared around the Cape Leeuwin off our port on the fourth day out of Fremantle. The swell gradually increased to 3 meters, with a wind strength of 20 knots. It was a buzz for me sailing in these conditions, reefed down in a big ocean swell on a great little yacht with an obviously very experienced skipper.

FOUR SEASONS IN A DAY.

Robin and I were working well together. The sun was out, and despite all the hold-ups, Lotus 2 was making slow but steady progress along the coast. Albany was still over a hundred miles away, and only a couple of days left before

Christmas. There was still a good chance we could make it. Then I thought luck was really on our side when the fresh southerly suddenly changed direction and clocked around behind us to a westerly, precisely what we needed to get us into Albany on time. But my glee was short-lived when Robin pointed out an ominous cloud bank rolling in along with the westerly. The sky quickly darkened above us, and the first heavy drops of rain splattered down on the deck of Lotus 2. Robin went below and came back up with our wet weather gear, turned, and said, "Now you know why the locals who live along this coast say, 'four seasons in a day.' The rain became blinding, along with the wind, but I was happy. Lotus 2 was reefed down and romping along in the right direction. Robin was navigating with his Merlin navigational computer. (GPS was just starting to become available to the general public) Based on his boat speed calculations, Robin reckoned we would be approaching Albany and arrive around late afternoon on our sixth day out from Fremantle. Then he said, "I don't want to disappoint you, JJ, but we can't make the approaches in these conditions without an engine; we have to stay outside and wait until we have clear visual marks that we can see to navigate." It looked like the weather and time had beaten us - a Christmas Eve like no other! While we were both crawling around on deck setting up the storm sail for the night, I thought about what my friends in Perth were probably doing back in the city on Christmas Eve - another world! Once we had the storm sail correctly rigged, we could hove-to for the night in the driving wind and rain. It was a truly miserable night, but by first light on Christmas Day, the westerly had blown out, the clouds were breaking up, and the morning sun's rays were piercing through a grey dawn.

THE CHRISTMAS FISH

Up until that time, I hadn't thought about fishing. But now, with the sun warming the day, Robin happy at the helm for the run home, and a clear view along the coast towards Flinders Point, I had plenty of time to set up a 50-kilo hand line with a tuna lure on the end. The lure had only hit the water for a minute or so when my line suddenly snapped tight, and something big broke out of the sea 30 meters behind us. Robin said, "Better grab your gloves, JJ. I think you're going to need them." All my previous fishing had been done with a rod and nothing of any memorable size, so this was the first big fish I had ever hooked - an adrenaline rush! It's one hell of an experience pulling in a 10-kilo bluefin tuna hand over hand. I had to brace myself against the boat as the fish made deep runs, but slowly, I won out and finally managed to haul it over the stern. It was around a meter long and caused a real commotion, thrashing around in the confines of our small cockpit and getting all tangled up in the fishing line until I gave it a solid whack on the head with a hammer.

Twenty minutes later, we were closing the approaches, and just as Robin had predicted, the rock, aptly named Bald Head, broke through the surface, water streaming off its smooth sides resembling the top of a gigantic pink mushroom and posing a danger to any unsuspecting boat. Once past the leads, we sailed around Flinders Point and into the spectacular King George Sound. Finally, we found ourselves in sheltered waters, cruising past the smooth granite cliffs that encircle the point, and then into the vast Albany Harbour.

ALBANY. CHRISTMAS DAY '91
Around 10 a.m. Christmas morning, Robin brought

Lotus 2 up alongside the Albany town jetty. We had made it, and just as we came to a stop, a bunch of excited kids came running down to the landing with their new Christmas fishing rods. One of the boys took a mooring line for us, and they all wished us Merry Christmas. The boys were full of questions, wanting to know where we had come from and how long we had been at sea. Once the kids' curiosity was satisfied, they were off baiting up their lines, when I had an idea. I had cleaned our catch on the way into the sound and wrapped it in a wet towel, but the tuna was going to be a problem for us. We planned to spend the night in Albany at the farmer's place, then bus it home on Boxing Day. Carting a big wet fish around with us was going to be awkward and smelly, so I called one of the boys over, who was sitting on the edge of the jetty with his rod. He was around 8 or 9 years old. I asked him if he was getting any bites. "No, not yet," he replied, so I said, "Hang on a minute. I've got a surprise for you guys." I ducked down below and came back up with the tuna. His eyes nearly popped out when I unwrapped the towel around the fish and said, "How would you guys like to take this tuna home for Christmas?" His mouth dropped. He couldn't believe it. He let out a yell and called his mates over. They all crowded around, and I handed the fish to them, still wrapped in the towel. What happened next brought a smile to Robin's face and a lump in my throat. The boys all stood in a line on the jetty alongside Lotus 2 and started singing Christmas carols to Robin and me—a truly magical experience for the memory bank.

That ended the boys' fishing for the day. They wanted to get home with their prize tuna and a great Christmas story to tell Mum and Dad. The boys wished us a Merry Christmas again and thanked us for the tuna, then quickly disappeared. Robin found a phone box at the end of the jetty (pre-mobile) and rang the farmer. He was immediately on the way, and 20 minutes later he joined us on board, happy to see Lotus 2 in one piece. We briefly went over the voyage down with him. He was initially puzzled when Robin told him about the engine failure after only 100 miles of motoring. "Oh, sorry, did I forget to tell you that there was another hundred miles of fuel in Jerry cans under sails in the forward locker?" I won't print what I thought! We stayed at the farmer's house for the night and enjoyed a pleasant Christmas dinner with the farmer and his wife. He had pre-booked the bus for our return to Perth the following morning. Everybody was happy. After handshakes and thanks, Robin received a cheque and our bus tickets. We boarded the bus, and away we went - job done. (The cheque bounced!) So, that was my first delivery experience. It wasn't all good, but it was life-changing for me. I was buzzing, hooked, and wanted more. That initial voyage sparked my thirst for open-ocean sailing.

As mentioned earlier, I was a racing crew member at the Fremantle Sailing Club. The America's Cup Challenge defence series took place there in the local waters of Cockburn Sound in 1987 after Allan Bond's yacht, Australia II, ended the longest winning streak in history—132 years. For a few short months, sleepy old Fremantle became the yachting centre of the Western world. These were also heady days for me, as I owned a local wine bar called The Stoned Crow. Unfortunately, when I sold the business in 1989, the new owners, an Asian hotel group, refused to settle at the eleventh hour, setting me on a path of litigation. At my first appointment with the solicitor, he warned me I was in for a fight: "These guys play hardball." The only way I would get my money would be if we could take them to court, and that process could take a year or more. I was not in a good place, with little cash, and of course, my partner grew tired of all the negatives. Forty-five years old, and I was back on my own again… an old cliché. Everything happens for a reason. The ocean and delivering yachts became my escape and a chance to refocus.

THE JOB "SNIZORT"

We had completed a couple of coastal deliveries and then the big one. I picked up the phone. It was Robin. "Hi, JJ, I just had an inquiry about an international delivery, Singapore back to Fremantle. Interested?" The job is a 53-foot steel ketch, Snizort, lying on a mooring in Punggol Point, Singapore.

This was the first week in April 1992. Luckily, and for the first time, I decided to keep a record of this new adventure. So I picked up a little black pocket diary, which was precisely what was needed at the time, and now, years later, it would prove invaluable.

Robin arranged our first meeting with Jeff, Snizort's owner, at the Fremantle Sailing Club. (The reason I am not using his real name will become self-evident) Anyway, after introductions, Jeff told us he was an engineer, and he had built Snizort.

The Roberts yacht designs are plan-built kit boats, some with a hard chine, meaning that the hull is fabricated from flat steel plates welded together along the edges, creating an angular type of hull, not the usual round yacht shape. Naturally, this hull type is much quicker to fabricate than the traditional round hull. Even so, this is a 30-ton yacht and a massive undertaking for anyone to take on. I was impressed. Jeff appeared pleasant, confident, and softly spoken. He looked around fifty-five or sixty, with an average build and a world-weary, tired look about his face. My initial impressions seemed very positive. Over a meal at the club, Jeff told us he had not only built Snizort but also improved the engineering and made some minor modifications to the design. I understood that when completed, Jeff sailed Snizort from Sydney with friends to

Singapore, a fantastic voyage. But like so many yachties who sail to Southeast Asia from Australia, they run out of time, money, or both, so the boat gets left on a mooring off one of the many islands around Singapore. A couple of days later, you're back at the office, thinking that as soon as possible, you'll return and get your boat home.

Then life happens. The other reality of getting a boat back to Australia is this: the people or friends you did the original trip with will all politely say, "I'd love to, but I just don't have the time. Flat out right now." Been there, done that!

Anyone planning to sail north up the east coast of Australia will find for a good part of the year the winds are favourable right through to the inside passage of the Great Barrier Reef. Upon reaching Cape York Peninsula at the very northern tip of Australia, the northeast trades pick up your yacht and carry you on a very pleasant journey west into the Timor Sea across the top of Australia to the port of Darwin. Sailing north you cruise through the spice islands of Timor and Flores, past Bali, and through the Lombok Straits. From there you sail north into the Java Sea, then west along the coast of Kalimantan, finally crossing northwest and into the South China Sea and arriving at your destination Singapore, just a few miles north of the equator. Exotic tropical islands, generally fair winds, and, believe me, a fabulous voyage.

Unfortunately, as they say in sailing terms, the return trip is on the nose, into the wind, at the best angle you can get. For the delivery crew, that usually means long hours at the helm. The boat and the crew can get a hammering, and that's the reason Jeff needed us. He had left Snizort over a year earlier in Singapore, and we would be the crew to bring Jeff's yacht back home to Australia. So far we had a good track record, and our little business idea is coming together nicely. We called ourselves JJJ's International Yacht Delivery - Robin Jeffries and me, JJ. This was my escape plan and a break from all the litigation hassles. As for the money, the deal was $1 per mile plus travel expenses and accommodation. Not a fortune, but yes, three thousand plus nautical miles of open ocean sailing and some very exotic locations sounded like a good deal to me.

The next few days, the pace really picked up - all the usual stuff to get ready for our trip. This meant buying a heap of charts, as this was a time when GPS navigation was still in its infancy. Expensive gear to buy, but essential for ocean navigation. Robin had recently purchased his first handheld GPS unit. He explained that we needed at least three satellites above the horizon for triangulation to get our position, which meant we could only receive a limited number of fixes a day. Another problem with the GPS was intermittent transmission, as the US-owned system was regularly shut down for military reasons. It took nearly three more years for the 31-satellite GPS program to be completed in 1995.

There is a compelling agreement among delivery skippers that it's not a good idea to do a delivery with the owner on board. The situation is this: you have the owner and the skipper, so who is calling the shots? Jeff told us in his cool, confident tone that he would be in command, having already made the journey. It was his boat, so ok by me! Days later, and right in the middle of our preparations to leave, I got a call from my solicitor. He told me what should have been good news. Due to a cancellation, my court hearing had been brought forward and rescheduled for the end of the month - a disaster. So suddenly, it looked like I wasn't going anywhere. I knew my baling out just as we were getting ready to leave would throw a massive spanner in the works. There was nothing I could do but apologise to Jeff and tell him that I needed to be in Perth at the end of the month for my court hearing. Flying to Singapore and the delivery all looked out of the question. The litigation anchor was still firmly hanging around my neck. Then Jeff surprised me and came up with this idea. We all fly to Singapore and start getting the boat together. (Apparently, there was a ton of work to be done.) Then, I fly back to Perth at my expense. Presuming the court case was resolved, Jeff would pay my fare back to rejoin Snizort. He figured by that time there would be a number of parts needed for the boat, so I could do my court thing, then locate and return with whatever parts were needed for Snizort. This was expensive, but Jeff had the chequebook out. Great! I was going again, and everybody was happy.

SINGAPORE

I won't repeat a daily monologue from the diary, just highlight some of the more interesting days or feelings at the time.

Six a.m., and we were on our way to Singapore via Royal Brunei Air. After landing in Brunei, we faced a four-hour wait in a vast empty terminal with no other planes arriving or departing, and no alcohol was allowed - Muslim law! We finally arrived at Changi terminal in Singapore at eight p.m. After customs we decided to celebrate our arrival with a couple of drinks. We took a cab to Bugis Street, the old red-light district of Singapore. A sense of impending adventure had us all pumped up. We had a great night, and it felt like we were starting to come together as a team. We drank way too much and ended up with thumping hangovers the following morning. Not a brilliant start to our first day, but there was a job to be done, so after a coffee, we caught a cab into Changi to pick up some paperwork, then on to Punggol Point, where Snizort was waiting for us on a mooring a couple of hundred meters offshore. From that distance, she looked impressive with her big white hull and two tall masts.

PUNGGOL POINT. SNIZORT CENTER.

We had booked out of our accommodation at the Duke Hotel early that morning. Jeff's plan was for us to live on Snizort from now on. So, this would be our first night on board. Jeff had a Stacer 3-meter tinny (alloy dinghy) as a tender for Snizort. So, after arriving at Punggol Point, we made our way down to the boat ramp, launched the tinny, then piled in with our cleaning gear and were on our way. But as we drew closer to Snizort, the effects of being left anchored in the Straights of Johor for over a year really started to show. I don't think Jeff ever said exactly how long ago it was, but I had never seen a yacht that size in such a dilapidated state. I did take some before and after pictures, but that was another roll that didn't survive. Snizort was looking very sad and neglected. The constant humidity and extremely high rainfall turn everything damp and mouldy. As we pulled alongside and then climbed on board, I could see rust was apparent everywhere, running down the steel hull and the coach roof. There were several areas with fungal growth, and the varnish and paint were peeling off everywhere. Once we managed to get on board and have a quick look around the deck, I noticed a few strange plants had started growing out of the centre cockpit floor behind the wheel (I thought it looked more like a garden box!). We had birds' nests on deck and in the boom sail covers. The sails were coated with bird guano and looked like they had gone rotten and mouldy yellow in the heat - not a great first impression! After we had finished checking out the deck layout, Jeff pulled out his keys to unlock the accommodation hatch. As the cover slid back, the warm, heavy smell of mouldy air drifted up to greet us. We descended the companionway into a big open saloon area two meters below the deck level. When I reflect on it now, I should have stopped and taken a reality check. The open-plan saloon-lounge area was only partially finished off. The floor was just covered with sheets of plywood—a very basic galley on the port side. A central console for a dual steering station was located in the middle of the saloon area. Although great to get down out of the weather, it would be impossible to see anything forward. The master's cabin area aft looked a little more finished, but I noticed that the interior hull walls were all white enamel painted, with no insulation or lining. After being sealed up for so long, some of the paint was peeling off and condensation and bright red rust was running down the metal walls. Other internal areas I could see were also affected by mould. The saloon lounge area was partitioned into another cabin on the port side, which would be Robin's berth. Moving forward through the main bulkhead door towards the bow revealed a large, open workshop area full of assorted tools and timber. Then, I spotted the pipe berth hanging on chains from the hull wall. You guessed it…my bunk! This wasn't the picture I had painted for myself back in Fremantle. Sleeping near the bow at sea means a lot of movement, and you can get airborne on a 53ft yacht ploughing into a swell.

SINGAPORE CHILLI CRAB

The job was enormous! We tried some switches, but nothing worked. There were a couple of solar panels connected, but our batteries were dead flat. There was a ton of mechanical and electrical work to be done below deck. Snizort was going to keep us all busy for a long time. Robin was having a good look around below, and then he turned and caught my eye. It was a raised eyebrow sort of look. I shrugged. It was too late to think about changing our minds now. We began cleaning up below, trying to make Snizort habitable again. Every hatch and vent we could find was opened. Snizort desperately needed some fresh air! After three sweaty hours, plus gallons of bleach and detergent, we agreed that we would move all the rest of our gear onto Snizort and spend our first night on board. It had been a really long, hot, and humid afternoon below deck, so we all jumped into the tinny and went back to Punggol Point to cool off with a couple of cold beers. Once back on land and sitting at a local bar, we discovered that as the day faded into night, Punggol Point was the famous home of Singapore Chilli Crab. Coach loads of people arrived there every evening. Just a sleepy little bay during the day, but once night fell it was party time. All lit up with lots of local food stalls and live music, so instead of the intended just a couple of drinks to finish our busy day, we ended up there till stumps. And yes, you haven't tasted Singapore Chilli Crab until you've been to Punggol Point. The crabs were absolutely the best. I still can't remember getting back to Snizort that first night, just waking up with another thumping hangover the next day. We were getting to know each other and having a few laughs. Generally, things were looking very positive... apart from the hangovers!

Naturally, Punggol Point became our base camp at the end of each day, and the scene of many serious discussions over cold beers. If we were going to sail out of Punggol Point anytime soon, the next few weeks would be intense. Our main engine, a 6-cylinder Perkins, was dead until we got a new bank of deep-cycle batteries. Thank God Jeff decided to buy a heavy-duty Honda generator. We had an endless list of mechanical and electrical problems below deck, but that was not my department. I was topside, scraping and rubbing down, varnishing, painting the hull, fixing the sails, and getting some new ones made—all the wire rigging needed tension checking, navigation lights, frozen winches to repair, etc. The temperature hovered around 30 degrees all day, the air sticky and humid, especially around 4 pm with the inevitable monsoon downpour.

I spent one busy afternoon climbing both masts so we could install new navigation lights and replace the wind indicator. Doing so I found the radar scanner was frozen on the mizzen mast...a bit of a worry. From atop the main mast with my 35mm Minolta I took some photos of Snizort's deck fourteen meters below, where Jeff could be seen managing my safety lines.

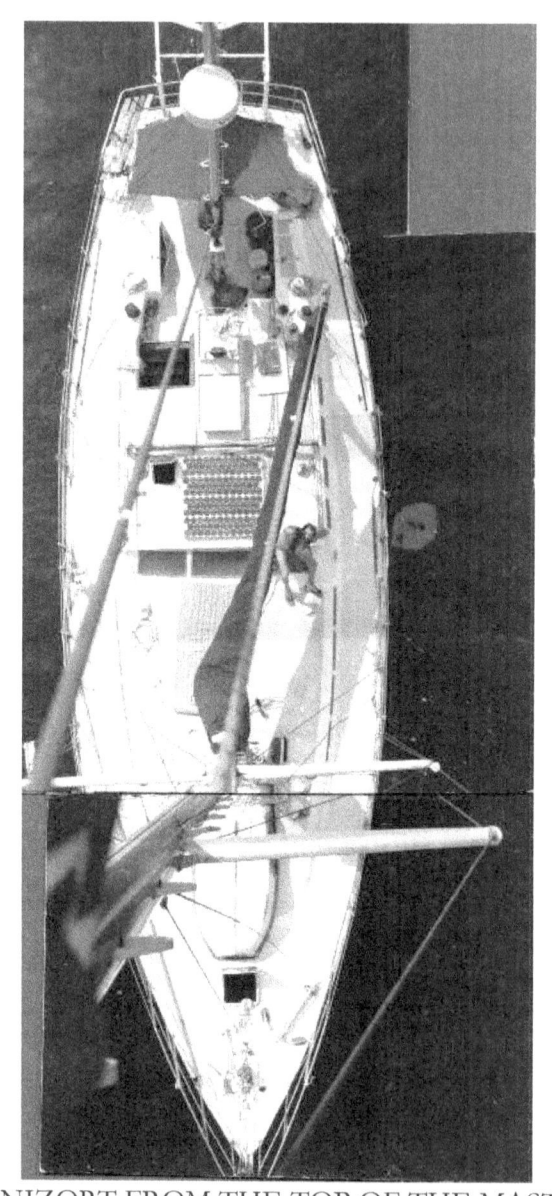

SNIZORT FROM THE TOP OF THE MAST

CLEANING THE HULL

Another major problem we had was below Snizort's waterline. As we pulled up alongside and tied up, I quickly looked down through the water on the side of the hull. The marine build-up was incredible. The growth was around half a meter or more, sprouting out from the hull walls. Schools of small fish were diving in and out of the seaweed-covered hull—a regular ecosystem!

The Straits of Johor is a narrow channel of water separating the Southern tip of Malaysia and the northeast coast of Singapore. Looking across the Straits to the southern coast of Malaysia from onboard Snizort, felt like we were anchored in a wide river. The surface was so polluted, with dead things floating past and an assortment of junk and plastic bottles. As we were only fifty or so kilometres north of the equator, the sea is naturally very warm, making a perfect recipe for marine growth. This marine buildup problem was also really my department.

Years before, in my twenties, I had worked as a commercial diver for several Australian marine construction companies, building jetties, subsea pipelines, and offshore platforms. I didn't have any dive gear with me apart from my face mask, so when I decided to get in, I first plugged my ears with cotton wool, a trick I had learned from previous experiences. There were a lot of little wiggly things that can get into every orifice. Oh man, when I first jumped in around the stern to take a closer look, I couldn't see anything other than a huge ball of marine growth a couple of meters or more across where the prop and rudder should have been. My initial idea that I could clean the 53-foot hull with a 4-inch paint scraper was ridiculous. When I climbed back on deck, my skin was crawling. Being bit of a hairy person, I had managed to collect all sorts of tiny prawns and sea fleas. That was it!

Snizort would have to come out onto the slip at the Changi sailing club, a few kilometres east along the coast from our mooring.

Jeff made some inquiries and found out that, yes, we could get her cleaned up and water blasted there. But, when he rang the club, he found that because of the condition of Snizort's hull, the cost would possibly be over $1,000 US. First, we would have the problem of getting Snizort to the club, which would mean a tow, unless we waited until we had engine power - catch 22! Then, a guy we had bumped into at the ship's chandler store suggested a local dive company that could help us. Jeff made a call, and two young guys came out with scuba gear the following morning. I really felt sorry for them. The visibility was zero once they started. The job took them all day. While cleaning the hull, the sea around Snizort turned into brown soup, boiling with fish. The divers scraped kilos of big green-lip mussels off the hull, but we didn't trust eating them as the water looked so polluted. Once they had finished, I decided to go for a dive and check out the end result. The hull didn't look anything like it did before, but it was still nowhere near clean enough to go sailing. Lots of furry bits were missed, which was understandable as the visibility was close to zero most of the time. Cleaning the hull sufficiently to sail could add up to 1 knot per hour and literally save a ton of fuel on a long ocean passage. So, I made it my mission to try and get Snizort's bum clean.

GOUT

Jeff and Robin drank all day, which is, I suppose, understandable. It was so hot and steamy. Initially, I had tried to keep up with them, but 9 years of running a bar had changed my ideas about starting the day with a cold beer. First, Jeff came down with the flu, then Robin had an attack of gout and had run out of his pills. Both his feet were swollen with uric acid inflammation. He was totally confined to his cabin and he couldn't get off his bunk, never mind the boat! Jeff sounded rough, still coughing and sneezing in his master's cabin in the stern, so I volunteered to see if I could get some medication in downtown Singapore. A good excuse to get away from the boat on my own for a day and some fresh air. Bus services are excellent around Singapore, so when I hopped on the downtown bus, a local soon directed me to the Central Public Clinic.

When I first arrived at the clinic, I discovered that the only way to see a doctor was to register as a patient there. Okay, so I filled out all the appropriate forms, registered at the clinic, and waited and waited. Eventually, it was my turn. "Hello, how can I help you?" he was a young Indian doctor, and when I tried to explain the reason why I was there, I could see he was scratching his head. He said, "You're not really a patient, are you? How can I prescribe medication for your friend that I have not even examined? I cannot do that". Then he offered me some Panadol, and I said, "We both know that Panadol is totally ineffective for treating gout." I had Robin's last box of medication and handed it to him. Then I said," Look, what if you prescribe the pills to me? We will only be here for a few more days. If Robin could possibly get off the boat and come to your surgery, he would be here!" I was becoming a problem, and I could sense that he wanted to get rid of me. After some hesitation, he finally relented and gave me the script in my name. But only after I promised him that we would be leaving Singapore in less than a week, never to return. Robin was more than grateful when I returned with his medication.

CALL HOME

Before leaving, I had made prior arrangements with my solicitor to keep me up to date and maintain regular phone contact (pre-internet days). I was in the process of buying my return flight when I thought to check with him before I purchased the actual ticket, and bingo, he told me that the court hearing had been adjourned with no fixed future date. What a relief! I was free and $560.00 richer. The rest of the crew was not doing so well. Robin was limping around, slowly recovering from gout, and Jeff was still down with the flu and drinking rum, making him very sullen. Still, he was happy to hear that I didn't need to leave. It seemed at the time I was the only one getting on with Snizort, but she was slowly starting to come together. The topsides were beginning to look a little more respectable, but there was still plenty of scraping and painting. The sails that could be repaired were ashore being fixed, along with a couple of new ones on the way. Life for me had definitely taken a turn for the better.

When I compared my work program to Jeff and Robin's job, down below decks every day in the oven-like heat of the engine room, I certainly didn't envy them. On the other hand, I was working topside, which meant I could simply jump over the side any time I felt the heat getting to me, cool off, and spend half an hour cleaning the hull. I was having a ball, messing around on a big ocean-going yacht in a foreign port. My lot in life seemed to be working out ok for a change.

ROBIN'S 50TH BIRTHDAY

April 24th diary entry:
"Today is Robin's birthday. Over the past few days, we have made good progress, and things are starting to fall into place. Jeff is much more cheerful and appears to have

recovered from the flu. Robin is back to his old self again, and since today is his birthday, we decided to call it a lay day."

After breakfast, I left Jeff and Robin to their own devices and headed downtown to see if I could find a gem store. Before we left Perth, I decided to bring along some West Australian gemstone samples. Lapidary was a part-time hobby of mine at the time. I wanted to see if I could swap my rocks for something interesting to take back to Aussie. When I finally located a gemstone store in downtown Singapore, I must have looked a little strange with my crumpled bag of rocks, very casual dress, and salt-encrusted shoes. The doorman, a huge guy who looked more like a well-dressed bouncer, blocked me as I went to enter. When I tried to explain what I wanted to do, he told me that they don't buy gemstones from the public and wouldn't even let me in. Not the sort of man I would argue with, so I was about to turn and leave when another guy came over from inside the store to see what was happening. He was much friendlier and said, "Well, let's look in the bag and see what he's got." The doorman stepped aside. My samples were rough, uncut, local, and unique to West Australian gemstones: Mookaite, Tiger's eye, and black Jade, weighing a couple of kilos or more. I figured they could be used in a display case, to place a necklace around, or something similar. The Mookaite was a blaze of red jasper and yellow mineralisation.

The rest of the afternoon was totally unexpected. I was taken through to the administration and introduced to the buyer. When I told him I just wanted to trade, not sell, he invited me into his office, where we sat down and talked rocks for a couple of hours. After a few very enjoyable glasses of chilled wine and nibbles, we completed a little trade: a beautiful Thai black star sapphire crystal and an uncut Thai ruby as big as my thumb for my rough gemstones. (When I passed by the store days later, right in the entrance to the foyer, next to the not-so-friendly doorman, there was a large display case window, and as I had imagined, my rocks were on display and draped with precious cut stones.) What a day! I made my way back to Punggol Point with my new rocks, feeling very pleased with myself. Later that afternoon, we all decided to head back downtown to Bugis Street for a meal to celebrate Robins's 50th birthday.

Robin originally grew up in the UK. He is a big-built guy, (slightly over 6ft 2"). sporting a full, greying beard. When I first met him, I thought he resembled a member of ZZ Top, or a Hell's Angel-type bikie, but I couldn't have been more wrong. Robin likes a drink but never seems to lose it. He doesn't chase after women, and is very polite and softly spoken. He also has a keen interest in ornithology and once studied under the guidance of the renowned UK conservationist Sir Peter Scott in his famous aviary - not your average yachty!

Back to our night out, while we were all sitting together having a few drinks, I spotted a hot female doing the rounds, going from table to table, asking guys if they would like some company. So, I left Jeff and Robin at the table, slipped over, and introduced myself. I explained my planned surprise for Robin's birthday to her. I pointed out the big guy with a beard. Then, I rejoined the crew. I expected her to come over a little while later, but instead, a much older woman suddenly appeared at our table, gave Robin a big smile, and wished him a happy birthday! I couldn't keep a straight face. Jeff and I started cracking up. Robin was more than a little embarrassed and quite indignant. Needless to say, he didn't fall in love. The rest of the night was over-the-top, full of laughs. It was easily our best day in Singapore.

THE GUN

Jeff announced one morning that he had left a military-style rifle with the Singapore police. The gun had been declared on his previous arrival and was held by the police in quarantine. Now, he wanted to retrieve it. I have spoken to several people about guns on boats and have concluded that it's a total loser. If you pick up a gun and point it at anyone, you have just given the person at the other end of the barrel a license to kill you in self-defence. Jeff was concerned about pirates in the Straits of Malacca and around the northern tip of Sumatra. He was doing the macho thing. "Just let them try" - not what I wanted to hear. As I recall, when a fishing boat tries to come close alongside, 99% are just local guys, honestly trying to sell something, waving fish around or cartons of cigarettes, with big smiles, happy, friendly fishermen. However, there could be the opportunist holding up a carton of smokes, with a pang (machete) tied behind his back, checking the number of people on board. His skipper in the wheelhouse would closely watch everything, keeping a high-powered weapon handy, just in case. If you start a war with one boat, remember that there are hundreds of others along the coast, and they all talk to each other on their radios. Come up with a gun, then you had better have the stomach for an actual shooting match—bullet holes in the boat or you.

SEAMASTER

The tragic loss of Sir Peter Blake, the New Zealand International yachtsman and environmentalist who lost his life in 2001, is a perfect example of what happens when you come up with a gun and pull the trigger without thinking of what happens next.

Seamaster, Blakes's 119ft expedition vessel, a specialised super yacht that was built initially for the Antarctic, had just finished a 3-month survey into the overfishing of the Amazon River basin. It was anchored a couple of kilometres offshore in the river overnight, near the town of Macapa in the mouth of the Amazon. According to one of the crew of 9, it was pitch black, with no external lighting. They were sitting around in the dark, talking on the rear deck and having a few beers, when a local gang of 6 thugs called the 'River Rats' thought the Seamaster would be easy pickings, full of rich tourists. Not expecting any opposition, the armed gang led by 20-year-old Rubens da Souza boarded the Seamaster and easily overpowered the crew. However, they didn't see Blake, who had managed to slip away below deck and grab his rifle. When one of the gang members, Riccardo Travers, went down into the accommodation, he encountered Blake coming back up. Blake fired instantly, shooting Travers in the hand and blowing off two of his fingers, but then Blake's rifle jammed. Travers automatically returned fire, shooting Blake twice in the back as he tried to turn around, killing him instantly. Immediately, the rest of the gang began firing, and the crew of the Seamaster dived down on the deck for cover. All the crew was then robbed. Watches, cameras, and some cash were taken before the 'River Rats' left, firing more shots into the hull of Seamaster as they made their getaway, with Blake the only fatality. The 'River Rats' gang were later all caught and sentenced to long prison terms. Travers was the longest sentence. 36 years in a Brazilian jail for shooting and killing Blake. At an in-depth interview with the press, the now infamous Travers asked for forgiveness and said, "It wasn't the end I planned. I'm sorry, I thought they were just rich tourists." It didn't have to end that way...a tragic death for only a few watches and some petty cash.

So, what were we to do about potential pirates? After a tip from another skipper, we would carry an ordinary plastic spray bottle. The spray would contain a mixture of bleach and hull cleaning fluid. It effectively removes marine growth and is quite a corrosive mix. Kept handy in the cockpit, with a range of two or three meters, just enough for a cockpit situation. It's not illegal, but if anyone were to get hit in the face with that fluid, their eyes and face would be on fire. The only thing a would-be pirate can do is jump off the boat into the sea, followed by a visit to the nearest emergency clinic. When a fishing boat comes right up alongside in the ocean, and attempts to put a line on, the first thing to do is to say a definite no, try to wave them off, and immediately change the direction of your boat. Secondly, and very importantly, if you have a camera handy, take plenty of pictures. Identification can lead to the confiscation of their boat by the naval authorities and the loss of their fishing license. Just like that, their livelihood finished forever, not really worth the risk for maybe a camera and a bit of gear or a few dollars cash on a yacht. We did hear about one pirate attack that was caught in the act by a patrol boat. The fisherman had his boat confiscated, which was then used for target practice in front of the entire fleet as a warning. I think they made their point! However, Jeff wanted his gun back, so he contacted the Singapore police with his receipt and, to my great relief, was informed that the weapon would need to be returned under police escort at a cost of $900 US. Jeff wasn't happy, and the gun remained with the Singapore police!

SNIZORT POWERS UP

Diary entry: "We have an engine; The Perkins is going!" After weeks of intense work, Jeff had finally managed to start the Perkins, our main engine. We were hoping everything that needed to be replaced or fixed was fixed. Around 10:00 am, our new batteries were connected, and bingo, after a few spins, the Perkins fired up with a couple of rattles and lots of smoke, then settled down to a steady beat, sounding quite good. We let her idle for a while to see if the cooling system and the heat exchanger were functioning correctly. The engine seemed to be idling sweetly. Visions immediately sprang into my head. - the straits of Malacca, sailing up around the top of Sumatra, then down to the Cocos Islands – it was really going to happen! We just had one more thing to do: engage the gearbox. There was a bit of a rumbling sound, then a loud bang. The Perkins was still running smoothly, but the prop shaft and the gearbox were frozen. Jeff instantly concluded that the prop bearing was probably seized. (We should have turned it manually!). As a result, the gearbox jammed, and then a shear pin had gone. Oh no! Initially, I thought the gearbox would have to come out, which could be a major time-consuming hold-up. Then I started thinking again, 'here we go - I'm going to be stuck in this heat for another month, and I'm getting really pissed off with Punggol point.' I had renamed the place for obvious reasons: Polluted Point. There were times when I just had to get out of the water while trying to clean the hull, with all sorts of garbage floating past me. It made me think about all those crabs that we had eaten!

MOVING

But as luck would have it, I was wrong. The gearbox problem turned out to be easily fixed. The broken shear pin was obvious and easy to get at when the inspection plate came off. Robin and Jeff took off into Changi to find new gearbox shear pins, while I went for a dive to look at the bearing. There was still a significant amount of coral growth surrounding the seal where the prop shaft exits the hull. It needed to be cleaned up properly. After the dive, I made my way back down into the engine room. A big wrench with a pipe extension was applied to the prop shaft. Half a turn was enough to break the whole thing free. When the rest of the crew returned, we had an hour of sweaty work, then fired up the Perkins again, and this time, when we engaged the gearbox, the propeller spun freely. We've done it. Snizort is GO! High fives all around. We would still need to top up the galley and fuel up the next day. Then, after completing the sea trials, we planned to move Snizort down to the Changi Sailing Club for the remainder of the weekend. Our departure from Singapore and the sailing part of the delivery is planned to start on Monday. Changi is a very up-market marina. I wondered how we would fit in with all the 'beautiful people.'

So, this was to be our last night at Punggol Point. We have been based there for nearly three weeks, and the local people have been over the top, ever helpful and friendly. We ended up getting really hammered again, with lots of laughs and goodbyes to our friends and a last meal of chilly crab. At the end of the night, we managed to stagger back on board Snizort. After all the work we had put into the boat, the endless hours of cleaning, rigging, painting, and diving, Robin and Jeff, below deck day after day, in the heat of the engine room, Snizort had regained some of her former pride and appearance as smart, 53-foot seagoing cruising ketch. No one said as much, but I think we all felt a little bit proud and very, very drunk.

CHANGI SAILING CLUB

Our first task in the morning, after black coffee and Panadol, was to raise the anchor. It was a relief when the anchor winch worked the first time. Then came the long, slow process of cleaning up a year or so's accumulated growth on the anchor chain, a few links at a time. Without the high-pressure deck hose, the job would have taken forever. We didn't want slimy mud and smelly seaweed plastered all over the inside of the anchor locker, so every link was blasted. Two hours later, we were hosing down the anchor and then all the mud off the foredeck.

We were all in the cockpit, Jeff at the helm, as Snizort finally motored out of Punggol Point into the Straits of Johor and on into the main channel. Snizort was then put through sea trials, and surprisingly, all the major repair work seemed to have been successful, with only a couple of gauges not functioning.

Our next destination was a fuel-lighter barge around 40 meters long, anchored out in the channel. As we approached, I could see an accommodation area at the stern. I was amazed. It looked like a woman was living onboard with her kids, a dog, and a few pot plants to brighten the black steel walls! We tied up alongside the fuel lighter, and the guy standing next to the diesel pump was having a smoke right underneath the no-smoking sign – classic! I should have taken a pic. Nearly two tons of fuel were taken on board Snizort.

With our deck tanks all filled, we were on our way, motoring down to the Changi marina just 5 kilometres east along the coast. After contacting the Changi club Harbor master, he directed us to tie up at a jetty astern of Puff, the first real super yacht I had ever encountered close up and personal. Snizort looked a little humble in comparison, the poor country cousins here for the weekend! It was easy to see that it was an exclusive club for the uber-rich.

By the time we moored up and got all the paperwork out of the way, it was late afternoon. Jeff and Robin decided to head into town for a meal and spend the rest of the night in Singapore. I was more curious about the Changi Sailing Club on a Saturday night. I had heard that club membership there, even in the early 90s, was in the many thousands of US dollars. We were just a visiting cruising yacht for a couple of days.

As the day ended, I made my way into the club and parked myself at the front bar. Around 7 p.m., a local TV station crew arrived on the scene and set up their gear. A catwalk runway was prepared on top of the bar for a fashion parade. The place quickly filled, and I found myself at the centre of a party for the affluent young Singaporean scene. Then I bumped into another Aussie skipper called Andrew. He was in charge of a fantastic yacht (I can't remember the name) that was being kept in storage at the club. What a job! Getting paid to live in the Changi Marina on a super yacht! After we had a couple of drinks, he asked me if I would like to have a look around the boat and said, "It's OK, I'm it - there's no one else aboard but me." We left the noise of the club bar, and then a short walk along the marina jetty brought us up to the stern of a gleaming black 40 meters of luxury.

THE UNTOUCHABLES

Andrew said that the yacht belonged to one of the owners of the Mahout heavy-lift shipping company. As we made our way up the on-ramp, Andrew asked me if I would like a smoke, put his hand in his pocket and pulled out a block of hash. I was surprised but smiled and said, "Are you kidding? It's the death penalty for drugs in Singapore. Aren't you a bit worried?" Andrew shook his head. "No, it's okay; the club has its own internal security. The Singapore police never enter the club. We are the untouchables!" So, we had a couple of pipes together and got smashed sitting on the bridge, surrounded by soft blue console lighting. Then Andrew took me on a tour of another world, an eerily quiet, floating palace. There was even a casino room in the stern, and naturally, Andrew was also the croupier. He told me he had been alone on board in caretaker mode for months and how bored he was.

Andrew asked me if I felt like going out nightclubbing or hitting the town. Nice of him to ask, but I just didn't have deep enough pockets for Singapore nightlife. It would have been fun, but I had to say no and retreat from the party life and super yachts to my modest bunk on Snizort and back to reality. I couldn't really complain.

Robin and Jeff rolled in hours later, and it sounded like they had had a big night. The following morning, after a lazy breakfast, Robin told Jeff that beer on Cocos was super expensive and sometimes just not available at all, so after a quick calculation, twenty-plus cartons of duty-free beer were ordered. An hour later, a pallet of cartons arrived at the jetty, and we started stowing them all onboard. There's a lot of storage space on a 54-foot yacht. While we were loading the beer below, I discovered many of the lockers were already full of cartons of red and white wine. Jeff also had a personal stash of rum in his master's cabin. So much booze, but it seems to be an absolute necessity in the tropics when you start the day with a cold one!

DAY ONE. UNDERWAY.

Our last day was filled with last-minute jobs. We topped up our fresh water tanks and picked up several cartons of bottled water. Jeff was happy, and we all felt Snizort was up for the voyage back to Aussie. We were on our way. At the day's end, Robin and Jeff headed back downtown again for a last night out in Singapore. I decided to stay on board. Getting smashed the night before the start of a big trip didn't work for me. Plus, I had one last night with Snizort all to myself. I was up early the following day. I felt great and ready to go, so I made breakfast for the rest of the crew. Robin was not too bad, but Jeff was very hungover and not in a good mood.

Changi Sailing Club is situated on the Northeast end of Singapore island. Getting into the Straits of Malacca meant we had to motor sail clockwise around the island, heading east, following along the coast, then south and finally west under Singapore.

Snizort pulled out of Changi around 10 am, then into Singapore's main harbour with a tropical downpour chasing us into the shipping channel. What an incredible sight! There were hundreds of capital ships, some moored, others coming and going in all directions, lots of brightly painted ferries, tugboats supply vessels, and Harbor pilot boats running back and forth. It must have been a nightmare of organisation for the harbour master.

Later in the day, we motored for hours through idle offshore oilfield gear - megabucks worth of gigantic floating cranes, jack-up rigs, and pipe-laying barges all waiting for a job in the heat. They brought back vivid memories of the years when I worked on similar rigs offshore.

Our next heading was southwest into the Singapore Straits with ships all around us. Then we turned westerly and after motoring all day finally passed the Raffles lighthouse. We started to enter the bottom of the Straits of Malacca at dusk. Navigation lights began to come on all around us. The GPS screen read that we were just a few miles north of the equator. Robin was busy with the charts, and Jeff was at the helm in a black mood and sounded like he had another cold. We decided to split the watches into four-hour shifts. Having three crew meant we got an 8-hour break between watches, and during daylight hours, we would be mostly all on deck. Also, we had an autopilot, which should have made life easy. I volunteered to do my first watch from 4:00 a.m. to 8:00 a.m., so after cooking our evening meal, my bunk was calling.

STRAIGHTS OF MALACA

I hadn't slept much. Apprehension and a spoonful of adrenaline kept me awake, as well as the noise of waves hitting the hull outside my bunk and echoing through Snizort. My first watch was at 4:00 a.m. Most people hate the 'Dog Watch', but sunrise at sea can be so special. It was also the best time of day for setting up the fishing gear. Then there was that feeling like I had the boat all to myself, plus my Sony Walkman with great music, the rest of the crew all asleep…magic! The harsh reality was when at 3:45 a.m. Robin stuck a cup of coffee into my hand and said, "Morning, ready to go?" Once I got my act together, he carefully explained our position at the chart table. This position must be entered accurately into the ship's log at every change of watch, and the bilges are also checked in case of any leaks. The weather conditions and barometric pressure must also be entered. At the end of a delivery, it is standard practice for the skipper to hand the ship's logbook over to the vessel's owner.

The sightings of other vessels should also be included in the log, but it was bit pointless in the Straits of Malacca as the capital ship traffic is endless. On our paper charts, the shipping lanes, as they are called, were clearly defined and marked with north and south directions - like a freeway! Small private vessels, like Snizort, tugs and barges, must steer clear of the main shipping channels and hug the coast.

Once the fog in my brain had cleared, I climbed up into the cockpit behind the helm. Only then, after a quick look around, could I fully appreciate what was going on. Lucky for me, we were motoring north with the autopilot on, no wind, no sails to adjust, pretty much flat water, lots of navigation lights, and capital ships over on the port side, but no problems holding the course or staying on deck. Snizort was humming along in the tropical night air. I had an intense feeling that this trip was going to be huge.

Not long before dawn, 100 kilometres north along the Malay coast from the bottom end of the Straits, we cruised past the lit-up port of Melaka. Melaka is also purported to be the home of the original Buggies Pirates, so you could say I was a little bit on edge as the term "The bogeyman will get you;" originated from this area. The Straits of Malacca have had a notorious reputation for piracy from the 14th century to the present day. So, I was keeping an eye out for any strange lights approaching. Several fishing boats were leaving the port, getting an early start, but thankfully, not heading my way. Nothing unusual was sighted.

The Malaysian government had several high-speed patrol boats built in Australia and armed with a 50 mm cannon, so we had been told not to worry about a pirate attack. The problem for us was the patrol boats were generally out in the shipping lanes looking after the capital ships, not inshore along the eight hundred kilometres of coastline where the attacks typically occurred. Snizort now joined the fishing boats, barges, and ferries as part of that coastal fleet.

When dawn finally arrived, it was time to rig up the fishing gear. Just a spoon-type lure about 30 meters astern, attached with a bungee shock cord does the job every time. Once the sun came up, I livened up a bit. By 8:00 a.m. at the end of my watch I felt sandy-eyed but wide awake. I let Jeff have a sleep-in and put the kettle on. It was time for some breakfast. Robin got up first and we started planning the next stage of our trip together over a cup of tea. So far, so good! No fish yet!

4 DEGREES NORTH

A little over one month away from home, and we were nearly halfway up the Straits of Malacca. Early the next day, Robin pulled in a barracuda that was almost a meter long. I had left the gear out when I went off watch; the lure spinning away behind the boat, when bang - now we had beautiful fresh fish. Robin and I were having a great time. Unfortunately, Jeff wasn't feeling the same and not happy. Then, while I was on watch early in the evening, Jeff entered the cockpit. We were having a conversation about our journey, when he told me how he gets really bored with ocean sailing. That really surprised me. Before we left Singapore, he often reminisced about his great voyage north from Australia and how getting into the ethos of sailing had changed his life. Now, he didn't seem to be able to relax and get into the trip. It always takes a couple of days at sea to let go of the beach and adjust to life on board. We still had thousands of miles of hard sailing ahead of us! I couldn't figure out why he was even doing all this. I thought, if that's how he really feels about ocean sailing, why didn't he just get Snizort ready for the voyage and then leave Robin and me to do the delivery part?

LUMUT

Around 3 pm, after motoring north all day along the coast, still in the straights, we pulled into the port city of Lumut, 4 degrees north on the banks of the Dinding River. There was a lot of traffic and a couple of big islands around the entrance to the river mouth. Luckily for us, Robin had visited the place before. There seemed to be docks and small jetties for miles along the banks before we reached our destination—the Lumut Marina, which turned out to be a surprise.

As we approached, it had the appearance of a very upmarket complex, with floating jetties and all the modern facilities. But after we tied up alongside the main jetty and looked inside one of the metal bollards that are supposed to house the power and water outlets, we found nothing, no water or power. Seemingly they hadn't got around to that bit yet. I thought it was funny and typical of a lot of unfinished infrastructure projects in Southeast Asia, but Jeff was really pissed off. We had to organise a long hose and a power lead all the way back down to the main jetty.

The Marina clubhouse was a nice new building, but apart from a couple of people in the bar area, the whole place looked deserted. I figured they were really struggling financially. Very little was happening around the place. Other than Snizort, only two or three other boats were in the marina, leaving a couple of hundred empty boat pens. As we walked down the central jetty, I looked up at the flags flying on poles over the clubhouse. Robin pointed out the jellyfish logo on them and reckoned that the jellyfish in the river mouth could grow to an enormous size. He told me of an incident on another delivery when a huge jelly got tangled up in the dinghy anchor chain. He said he had to get half out of the dinghy and then stand on the dome of the jellyfish to push it free of the chain. It was a monster jelly, nearly big enough to support the weight of a man! Fortunately for us, not a stinging variety. I looked for them but didn't see anything near that size.

PROPOSITIONED

Later that day, once all the necessary mooring jobs were completed, we headed back down to the marina bar. Robin and Jeff were settling into the clubhouse for the night, so I had a beer with them and then decided to have a walk into downtown Lumut. By this time, it was around 7.30 p.m. Lumut didn't look like it had a big population, my guess just a few thousand people. After leaving the marina area, I didn't see another European, no women and only a couple of men in casual Western-style clothes. I noticed that as I approached, they would all lower their head and step to one side out of my way.

Eventually, I came across a bar and wandered in. I had just ordered a drink when a young Malay guy introduced himself and told me he was a hairdresser, and would I mind talking to him as he wanted to practice his English. I gathered that not many tourists visit Lumut. I suppose I was a little bit slow, but the back of his hand gently resting against my knee was an instant wake-up call. When I made it absolutely clear that I was only batting for the opposition, he quickly apologised and hoped that I wasn't offended. He then went on to tell me how hard it was for young people to meet one another in Malaysia. A family member must always chaperone single girls. Then he said, because he was gay, if we were caught together, he would be thrown onto sharp sticks, and I could face prison as an infidel! I am sure the last bit of the conversation was just in case I said something. I assured him that scenario was never ever going to happen. I finished my drink and decided to head back to the safety of the marina to catch up with the rest of the crew. This was one problem too many for a Fremantle boy!

THE DOG

Our original two-day stop in Lumut turned into five after bacterial-contaminated fuel blocked up our diesel filters. We had to order more spare filters and a fuel treatment kit for our tanks and then wait. Some other minor problems had to be taken care of regarding the Malaysian cruising permit, something we had missed in Singapore, so there were a couple of trips into the customs building in Lumut. Robin and I just dealt with all the little problems as they happened. Jeff got really pissed off with all the holdups, but that's the way it goes. He sat in the club bar for a couple of days in a foul mood. There was nothing we could do but wait until our filters arrived. Robin, as usual, knew a couple of local people who invited us into their homes for a meal. Everyone we met in Lumut seemed very friendly. Some were just a little too friendly!

Lumut wasn't a bad place to get stuck for a few days, but we were all eager to get going. Snizort finally cleared out of the marina on day five, just before lunch. A monsoon deluge hit us as we made our way north past a couple of islands and back into the Malacca Strait's main channel. Visibility was down to a few meters, and we were right in the middle of the navigation channel when the bows of a big fishing boat appeared out of the tropical downpour, heading straight at us. Luckily, we were both going dead slow and slid past each other safely port to port, the fishermen hanging over the side, all waving madly in the tropical rain. Then, as the rain started to ease, we saw the strangest thing. A big dog appeared to be standing on the water ahead of us near the river mouth. As we drew closer, I could see the dog was highly anxious, standing on top of a small pontoon around a meter or so wide. Every time a boat passed, the wake made the pontoon jump around, and the dog was doing a balancing act trying to stay on top. I couldn't see any food or water for it. "It's the fishermen," Robin said, "They leave their dogs on the floats overnight to protect the crab pots from poachers." A dog's life!

My first watch on this leg of our journey began at midnight. After doing the log with Robin, I climbed up into the cockpit and settled in behind the helm. When I looked ahead to the north, the horizon glittered with the boom lights from hundreds of squid boats on a glassy sea. Above me in the night sky, lightning flashed beneath the clouds, but there was no thunder, no wind, and apart from the throb of Snizort's exhaust, no noise -a surreal sight and feeling in the warm night air. This was the sort of experience that I had hoped for and imagined before leaving Oz.

LANGKAWI - EAGLE ISLAND

Langkawi, our next destination, is a duty-free island situated on the Thai- border. Locally known as Eagle Island, it is located 120 nautical miles north of Lumut along the Malaysian coast. This was our last stop before heading west across the straits and over the top of Sumatra. As we approached Langkawi from the south, the mountain in the central part of the island gradually emerged from the sea before us, eventually towering thousands of feet above us as we navigated the entrance channel between a group of small, picturesque islands covered in dense jungle. The channel then opened out into the Bass Harbour Marina, with the backdrop of the mountains behind, providing a stunning setting. Tropical islands surrounded us as we motored into the anchorage area.

The marina, a truly world-class facility. was a project personally sponsored by Malaysian Prime Minister of the day Mahathir. The island takes its nickname from the famous sea eagles: huge majestic black birds crowned with a white-crested head and neck, and a mean bright yellow beak out front. They circled lazily overhead like vultures as we tied up alongside the Langkawi marina clubhouse. Over the next couple of days, we had to focus on fully preparing Snizort for the trip to the Cocos Keeling Islands. This voyage must be completed in one hit, no more one-day trips or overnight stops. Once we left Langkawi, it would be 1300 nautical miles nonstop. Our course would take us over the top of Sumatra, and then down to Cocos. If we' were lucky enough to average a speed of five knots, it would take us a couple of weeks.

Jeff and Robin were planning to go into town to find the spare parts and other bits and pieces for Snizort, and I needed to go to the markets to organise the food and drink for the next two and a half weeks. I also would have to allow an additional 10% for any unforeseen delays.

APPROACHING LANGKAWI

ZACK

Once we had moored up and cleared in, a drink at the Marina Club bar seemed to be in order. While we were settling in and having our first well-earned beer, I met Zack, who introduced himself to me with his business card as a 'personal agent'. I'm sure these guys hang around the bar, and when they see a likely customer, it all just flows from an introduction and a couple of drinks. Zack had a car and offered to take me into town and help me get all our stores and provisions. So, yes, it's a good deal in a strange port; - an agent can save you a hell of a lot of time. No money was initially mentioned, but we all know there's no such thing as a free lunch, so a handshake will do. We finished our drinks and left the bar, then I was introduced to Zach's transport, a little old English Morris. First, we had a bit of fun. Zack wanted to show me around Langkawi, so he took me out of town to some places that I guess no tourist would ever typically see. I had to laugh when we arrived at his friend's clothing shop, which was brightly signed 'Fook Hin Smart Centre.' Next, Zack promised to show me the best view in Langkawi. We jumped back into his car and made our way onto a road that snaked 8 kilometres to the top of the mountain. At nearly 1,000 meters, and well above the clouds. I was beginning to think Zack's struggling engine wouldn't make it. The road ended close to the peak alongside a beautiful wooden-clad restaurant called the Eagles Nest, but it was closed, all shuttered up. Zack took me around to the lookout platform. The vista from the top, looking down through the clouds to the bay where Snizort was anchored, was breathtaking. Zack wasn't wrong about this being the best view on the island. There was only one other tourist couple on the platform at the time. I said hello to them, then decided to see if I could capture the amazing view. When I discovered that I had run out of film. I reloaded the Minolta and shot off half a roll. Unfortunately, another bunch of pics that would have a watery end.

FOOK HIN SMART CENTER

The Eagles nest restaurant area looked bleak and deserted, a bitterly cold wind whistled around us, but a worthwhile break from the oppressive heat and humidity down at sea level. Zack explained to me how he hoped that President Mahathir would make Langkawi Island world famous, just like Bali, so that many international tourists would come and make him very rich. Zack also confided to me that he had three wives but wished he could afford another one.

After visiting the local supermarkets and packing Zack's little car to the max with our boxes and stores, we drove over to his mother's place for a meal. He wanted to proudly introduce me to his family and his new Australian friend, JJ. Sitting there with Mum and one of his wives cooking, I thought this had to be one of the best experiences of the trip so far. I knew Robin and Jeff would be wandering around town, having a few drinks and getting whatever was needed for Snizort, but I was having a fabulous home-cooked meal with the locals. The food was different and delicious, with lots of little dishes, unlike any other Asian food I had ever tasted before and served with Jasmin tea, the perfect complement.

When the meal was over, I thanked Mum and his lovely but overly polite and painfully shy wife for her hospitality (which wife I don't know!). We all stood up, and then everybody repeatedly bowed to each other. It was time to go and get back to Snizort in Zack's little car loaded with supplies. Once at the marina, all the stores needed to be transferred onboard Snizort alongside the main jetty. It had been a long and busy day, and we would need at least two more carloads of supplies, in addition to a visit to the fresh food markets. When Zack and I pulled into the jetty, Jeff and Robin were already onboard, back from town with their parts, so we all got stuck into it together. By the time everything was stowed away, we were all dripping wet in the heat. I thanked Zack and arranged for him to pick me up first thing in the morning.

After loading our stores, we agreed it was time to cool down and head back to the marina club bar, which sits atop a ritzy, glass-fronted building perched on the side of a hill, offering spectacular views overlooking Bass Harbor and the surrounding islands. There was a duty-free inter-island Ferry terminal right next door to the marina. Thousands of people from all over Southeast Asia arrive there every day to do their shopping and pick up some duty-free alcohol, creating a very busy and vibrant scene.

After a cold beer, I decided to go for an evening run around the edge of the circular quay. Very tall coconut trees bordered the esplanade. As I was jogging along, a coconut fell and just missed me with a thud. The palms were around 10 or 12 meters high. From that height, it could have easily fractured my skull or broken a collarbone, and that would have been the end of my trip. It was a close call. I decided to keep the coconut for good luck and took it back to Snizort.

LEAVING LANGKAWI

The Doldrums are a low-pressure area stretching from 6 degrees north to 6 degrees south of the equator, where there is very little sailing wind. This region is part of the intertropical zone. In the old days, this area was called the horse latitudes because the square-rigged sailing ships would be becalmed for weeks around these parts. The story goes that they would eventually have to throw horses overboard, as they require gallons of fresh water and a special diet. Horses were always kept on board as transport for the officers and for moving goods around ashore. So, they say the horses would only be dumped over the side in extreme circumstances as a last resort. Personally, I would have thought it would have made more sense just to eat them!

Snizort's decks are now lined with twenty jerrycans, all carefully tied to the handrail stanchions, in all about half a ton of diesel. Hopefully, enough extra fuel for our journey. I've heard it said that 'If you're going to go a long way, sailing is the only way'. It's impractical for most power boats to try and carry enough fuel to cross oceans unless you have a huge ship. Alongside the extra fuel, we also had another two freshwater containers tied on deck. In case they were required in an emergency abandon-ship-type situation, a very sharp knife was also taped to the tie ropes for obvious reasons. I decided to give Snizort a last check below the waterline the day before we left. While I was submerged, I swam into the trailing tentacles of a jellyfish. I didn't see it, but I sure felt it. I was quite badly stung, with blisters around my head, ears, and neck. Later that night, I had some weird dreams. There were whip-like burn marks on my skin for days after.

PATROL BOAT

We weighed anchor and slipped out of Bass Harbour around 2 p.m., heading west down the main channel surrounded by picturesque islands, some hundreds of feet high with gleaming black marble cliffs draped in dense green jungle cover. A massive ocean liner slowly edged its way in on the other side of the channel, heading into Bass Harbour. Close to three hours later, as the sun was getting low in the sky, we broke out of the shipping channel past a couple of islands and back into the Straits of Malacca. I turned around for one last look at Langkawi Island. The mountaintop was still catching the last rays of the sun as we motored into the fading light.

So far, we didn't have to worry about capital ships, as we hugged the Malaysian coast all the way from Singapore, managing to stay out of the main shipping channels. However, that situation had now changed significantly. Fishing boats, container ships, and tankers were coming from every direction, travelling north and south at different speeds. We had to carefully thread our way through one of the busiest shipping lanes in the world. Capital ships couldn't turn quickly enough to avoid us. I'm not even sure if we would have stood out on their radar among all the fishing boats at night. Snizort was just another blip on the screen.

We were all on deck together, taking in this incredible sight ahead of us, when I said, "This looks like a dangerous place to be fishing," Robin agreed and said, "Oh yes, sometimes ships arrive in Singapore with bits of fishing boat rigging or a mast hanging off the anchor." When ships appear on the horizon, they are about 10 to 15 kilometres away, depending on their height. Standing in the cockpit at the helm of Snizort, my eye level was roughly three meters above sea level. If we were on a collision course with a capital ship, that would have given us around 15 minutes to change our course, depending on the closing speed of the other vessel, which should give us plenty of time to manoeuvre. But if we became occupied elsewhere for a few minutes or were busy resetting the sails, a hairy situation could have developed very quickly. So, we maintained a constant lookout since entering the main shipping channel, keeping our eyes peeled.

We couldn't all stay on the lookout, so I prepared our evening meal and then collapsed into my bunk. I would be back on watch at midnight. A bit after 11-30p.m. Robin woke me up with a coffee. He told me that we had cleared the worst of the traffic in this area but to be alert, as "there are lots of squid fishing boats working around us." When I got on deck, some of the squid boats were just a few hundred meters away, their extended booms lit up out over the water. The blaze of light created a vision problem on a dead, flat sea. There was so much glare and surface reflection from the fishing boats that spotting the port or starboard navigation lights of big ships coming over the horizon at night was not easy. At the same time, in the distance, forked lightning could be seen flashing along the horizon. All this extra reflection was making the job of focusing my eyes in the tropical night extremely difficult. Robin stayed up in the cockpit for a few more minutes - maybe he sensed my apprehension. I was absorbed in the job ahead when he said, "JJ, if you're not sure, don't guess," and told me to wake him up anytime if I got confused. Eventually, I settled in behind the helm, my eyes straining as I looked ahead and behind, surrounded by lights everywhere. After a few minutes, I felt more comfortable and settled into my watch.

I guess Robin had only been gone for half an hour or so, and I was feeling quite relaxed when suddenly a powerful searchlight totally blinded me, and then I heard someone shouting in Malay over a PA system. Initially, I froze and then went to dive down into the shelter of the cockpit. Next thing, I heard the roar of their exhausts. At first, I thought this was it. Pirates! Thankfully I was wrong. By the time I could see through the glare of light, a patrol boat was right alongside us. I cut the engine and breathed a sigh of relief. Jeff and Robin were already up on deck to see what all the noise was about. After frightening the Christ out of me, the Customs officers were quite friendly and just wanted to check out our ID's and Cruising Permit. I guess we could have been smugglers. Once they had checked out our paperwork, they roared off again into the night, just doing their job. The rest of my watch was uneventful. Still, there was no wind. Snizort motored on through the tropical night, our course taking us west towards the northern tip of Sumatra and the Rondo Passage.

SUMATRAN SQUALL

We motor-sailed continuously after leaving Langkawi. The occasional monsoon squall was accompanied by wind and heavy rain, usually lasting for 15 minutes or so. We really needed to sail around 50% of the time to conserve fuel, otherwise, we won't make it to Cocos. So far, the local squalls provided only a half an hour or so of sailing time - if we were lucky. It was hardly worth the effort of pulling the sails up.

Ahead of us, perhaps 10 kilometres away, loomed a different, much larger cloud formation. A towering cumulus wall rose thousands of meters into the afternoon sky. Beneath it, a smooth, grey, rolling cloud edge faded to black, giving way to a silvery-white area at sea level. Robin didn't like the look of it and told us to prepare for a real Sumatran wind. 50, maybe 60 knots. Jeff and I quickly started clearing all the loose stuff off the deck. I checked all the tie-downs while watching the dark grey wall approach. Then I went below, and anything that could move was stowed away as fast as possible. Once back on deck, the grey-white squall line beneath the cloud was visible, rushing across the surface, lightning behind it. There was nowhere Snizort could run or hide, so we slowly pushed on under bare poles. Then, just when it seemed like we were going to get really hammered, the squall line appeared to slip away to the south of us. A blast of wind hit us. We quickly rolled out our headsail and took advantage of the sudden pressure, but the main part of the system completely missed us. We all thought we were very lucky, but it was a sign of things to come.

RONDO PASSAGE. ACEH.

Aceh lays at the northern tip of Sumatra and is a very mountainous area, with volcanic peaks rising some 1500 meters or more above the jungle. The icy, dense, and heavy air near the peaks can rush down the slopes to replace the warm air rising from the ocean surface. This phenomenon, called a katabatic wind, could pose significant dangers to us near to the coast, as this type of wind can be nearly impossible to predict and reach hurricane force winds of 60-70 knots. It can also appear very quickly, with little or no warning. The sails can be shredded, or the boat knocked down on its side in a matter of minutes. So, we stayed off about 20 kilometres north of the Aceh coast, heading for the Rondo Island passage. Unfortunately, this heading was also the lesser of two evils, as it placed us again in the shipping lanes. So, with no other options, we motored west through the endless stream of ships that needed to cross over the top of Sumatra in both directions to reach Singapore. All three of us were quite tense; no one spoke much. I think we all felt small and vulnerable amidst so much heavy traffic, especially at night.

While I was on the 8 p.m. watch, Jeff came up into the cockpit after our evening meal. He was in a friendly, reflective mood and told me how much he missed his rural property back in Australia and vowed never to leave it again once this trip was over. I sensed the sea was really getting to him. There wasn't much I could say, he was clearly not in the same headspace as Robin and me, and we still had at least a couple of weeks at sea ahead of us before we reached the Cocos Islands.

Snizort was motor sailing as we had the prevailing westerly wind right on the nose, and we needed to make a westward course to get over the top of Sumatra, so we were beating into it. Robin thought we should lay off the wind more to the northwest to conserve fuel, but Jeff wanted to push on. Snizort was like a bucking horse but felt rock solid in the rising sea. The wind slowly kept increasing, and when we checked the log at the end of Robin's watch, our position showed that we were not making much headway at all, just burning fuel. Jeff relented, and we dropped off to the northwest towards the Rondo Island light, an extinct volcanic peak, poking its top just 70 meters out of the sea. The tiny island light was only a few kilometres northwest of us. Once passed, we could alter course and head south into the Indian Ocean.

Eventually, we were in the busy passage between the most northerly island off the Aceh coast called Pula We Island and Rondo Island. The passage at this point was just 20 kilometres wide. Our sails were reefed down, and we had to motor sail to make any headway. There was nothing else we could have done, so this situation continued for another hour or so for the gain of only a few kilometres. I came on watch at 8 p.m. after Jeff. (Captain's watch for a change). He was not in a good mood and looked a bit unsteady. We had some sail adjusting to do before Jeff went to go below, but he lost his footing and fell down through the open hatch of the cockpit with a yell. I hurried down to help. Luckily, he had managed to hang on with one arm and was just bruised. There were some colourful expletives, but he was lucky there was no real damage other than to his pride. That's sailing! Things can go seriously wrong in an instant. The rest of my watch was miserable, with rain that became almost horizontal. The Force 7 westerly slowly clocked further north, which was ideal for us as we could then set a new course southwest, a heading that would put us back on track for the Cocos Keeling Islands.

What a relief it was for us to get out of the Aceh shipping lanes, and Snizort was showing us what she could do in an ocean swell on a beam reach. Finally, we no longer needed the diesel. Snizort was 100% powered by wind, and we could shut down the Perkins…silence after days and days. No more diesel exhaust fumes! There was still a lot of noise from the wind and waves echoing through the hull walls, but we were making over 7 knots under reefed sail, and for once, the breeze was in the right quarter, pushing Snizort south and bang on course for Cocos. The next couple of days seemed like one storm after another. I had given up trying to sleep in my bunk near the bow days earlier. I was spending more time in the air than in the bunk, so I decided to lay my mattress on the saloon floor, midships.

THE EQUATOR

We had sailed and motored over 500 kilometres south-southwest since rounding the top of Sumatra, making good progress despite the constant squalls, followed by days with little or no wind. The bad news was our autopilot had decided to quit, so now we were back to manually helming. Having a ketch rig (two masts) really helped in this situation. With a bit of a tweak every now and then on the mizen to balance the main, the ketch rig held its course better than a sloop rig would have. Still, the constant battle with the helm. in big seas presented a challenge.

The GPS told us we were only a few hours north of the Equator. Earlier in the day, the wind dropped off, so we were back in the doldrums, hot and steamy, motoring on an oily, flat sea. Then I got lucky with my fishing gear; my lure hooked a nice little yellowfin tuna just before lunch. Sushi…yum! As we approached the 00:00 line, it was time for a traditional celebration. Years before, I had crossed the line as a passenger on a cruise liner. Everyone gathered around the pool to celebrate with King Neptune. This time it was totally the opposite. It gave me a strange feeling of total isolation as we hadn't sighted any other vessels since clearing the Sumatran coast. We were truly in the middle of nowhere. However, reaching this point felt like a real achievement, and were all in a positive mood after crossing this milestone. We held a little get-together up in the cockpit, followed by drinks all around, and then some fresh sushi, with the help of our last lemon. The coconut that just missed me in Langkawi was turned into a 'Pina Colada' with the help of some powdered milk, a tin of pineapple chunks, and a bottle of rum. All it needed was a little umbrella and some ice.

After our meal we caught a bit of a breeze, our sails went back up, and Snizort finally slid over the Equator at 5 knots around 6 pm which happened to be on Robin's watch. A fine evening meal of fresh tuna steak, accompanied by a can of peas and powdered mashed potatoes was enjoyed by all. This had been one of those feel-good days onboard, and everybody seemed positive for a change. I had hoped earlier that we would cross in the daylight so I could get over the side and then swim over the line. That would have been fun - maybe next time.

We were back in the southern hemisphere and from then on, instead of reading decreasing numbers south, our GPS position would read ever- increasing degrees south as we sail away from the Equator. Cocos lay 12 degrees, or roughly 720 nautical miles, to the southwest of our position. We were halfway there. With a bit of luck another week of sailing would get us there.

CHASE THE WIND

I had thought earlier that for this part of the trip, being so close to the equator, we would have been just motoring on a flat sea, but for days we had isolated patches of wind, which kept bus sailing. At times ahead of us were towering cumulus clouds with rain squalls under them drifting over the glassy surface. If we motored over, sometimes we could pick up some breeze around the edges. There would be just enough wind to sail for an hour or so, then all sails would be flogging with no wind. The main sail was dropped and the headsail furled and the motor switched on. Other times we only ended up underneath a tropical downpour. In this stop - start manner we made our way south. All simple stuff, but it was stinking hot and humid, our liquor supply was taking a big hit, and we were all getting weary from the slow progress and constant work required to keep Snizort on course.

My watch was due to start at midnight after Jeff's. I had woken up early, around quarter to twelve. Everything seemed noticeably quiet, unlike the usual sound of the sea on the hull. We would generally get a wake-up call and a coffee from the previous watch. As I made my way back through the galley I came across Jeff. He was curled up on the floor at the bottom of the companionway. Initially, I thought maybe he had fallen again and hurt himself, so I went over to see if he was all right, but he rolled over on his back and started snoring. I just stepped over, left him there, and went up on deck. The sails were all backwinded. We were drifting, slipping sideways through the night. I got Robin up to help me get Snizort back on course. When Robin joined me in the cockpit, he noticed that a heavy swell was starting to build from the south, so he ducked back down below again to check the barometer. When Robin returned, he said, "The glass is falling. We had better keep a close eye on the weather. It looks like a fair bit of breeze will come behind that swell." By the time I finished my watch, the wind had already picked up to a steady 15 knots. Robin took over, and I went below to do the log. Jeff had disappeared into his cabin. It had been 11 days since we left Langkawi, and all our fresh food has gone. From now on it would be noodles, tinned food, and pancakes until we reached Cocos. Yum not!

ANGRY SEAS, ANGRY MEN

The next three days bore out Robin's predictions. I wrote "storms" across those pages in my diary. The truth was I didn't want to record all the crap that was going on between us. Jeff would get all wound up and for some reason, making derogatory remarks about our sailing capabilities. Robin and I were just trying to get on with the job. Jeff's mood swings would go through Jekyll and Hyde - like periods; one minute he was quite pleasant and easy going, the next minute angry with threatening behaviour, followed by silence and what seemed like deep depression. Knowing how to handle such a complex and conflicted personality was not easy.

The wind strength had increased again to force seven, 30 knots plus. Snizort was getting a hammering. We were hard on the wind trying to make headway south. Healed over, up one swell, surfing down the next, slamming through the seas; skies leaden grey, constant rain squalls, and everything wet.

While I was on watch after lunch, Jeff came up into the cockpit and told me he wanted to get a break from the weather, which meant we would have to pull away and run downwind with the swell for a while. We were reefed down, plus the mizzen sail was set. I said we would need to drop the mizzen and ease the gear if we were going to run off in these conditions. Jeff just told me to get out of the way and took over the helm. The next minute, all hell broke loose. Jeff spun the helm, and the bow dropped off the wind, but the next swell hit us hard and smashed the bow down. I went to ease the mainsheet, but the mizzen sail caught the breeze and pushed us back up into the weather. We were beam-on; the next swell rolled us further over. Snizort broached. With all the banging and sails crashing back and forth, Robin was immediately up on deck to see what was going on. Then Jeff totally lost it and said something like, "I'm paying you a-holes to sail this boat, so do it." Then he told Robin, who hadn't said a word up to that moment, that "The crew is to have no more alcohol." Under the circumstances, I thought that was a joke. I was still wrestling with the helm, trying to get Snizort back on the wind. Alcohol was the least of my problems. Jeff then disappeared below into his master's cabin. At that point in the trip, I really thought Jeff was becoming a liability to us all. It seemed to me that he was getting more unstable and depressed as the days passed. Whatever the situation, we still had to get Snizort to Cocos. Jeff didn't reappear on deck for the rest of the day. Robin thought we should prepare for just the two of us running Snizort.

LACERATED HAND

The wind eased up, and the swell dropped. Sailing conditions improved, but it was still blowing around 15 knots from the southeast. We were getting into the Trades, and Cocos lay directly ahead, right on the nose. Jeff had appeared back up on deck and nearly apologised. Robin and I had discussed Jeff's mood swings, and we both agreed he had a few issues going on, and it was not all just about the booze. But, as they say, 'we were all in the same boat'

Cocos was only a day or so sail from our position, but to get the best approach angle to the wind would mean lots of tacking. Robin thought we should do a full check on the condition of our sails and rigging before we hit the approach to Cocos, so I went forward to do an inspection of the head sail and the main. Both sails were showing signs of wear and tear after the constant storms, with lots of fraying. Jeff wanted to motor sail so we could make more speed to get there a little quicker. It was a good idea, but we used a lot of fuel pushing over the top of Sumatra. Now, our fuel tanks were very low, and we were down to just the extra fuel that we had lashed on deck. Robin and Jeff had a bit of a stand-off. Robin wanted to save the fuel for the final approach to Cocos and keep sailing, but Jeff wanted to motor-sail.

Ultimately, the decision was made for us. While they were debating the use of fuel, the wind suddenly sprung up to near-gale force. Trying to motor into that would have been totally futile. Cocos wasn't getting any closer, and we were struggling to make any headway at all into the rising sea. I tried to reduce the head sail as Robin brought Snizort up to the wind. The furler wound in a couple of turns when I pulled the line, and then the rope suddenly went slack in my hand. The headsail unwound and filled back out, so now we were way overpowered. The furler line had parted somewhere, so I went forward again, slowly following the line to the point of the break. The headsail furler sat on the bowsprit at the bottom of the leading edge of the headsail. The pulley rope had worn through and parted close to the drum furler, so we couldn't wind the sail back in to reduce the sail area. I made my way back to the cockpit and told Jeff that I needed a sharp knife to cut the frayed end of the rope and then rewind it around the furling drum. Not an easy job under those conditions. I had no idea why, but Jeff suddenly said, "I'll get the knife and do the job myself." It was his boat, so off he went along the deck with his knife towards the bow, which was crashing through the sea. There was only room for one on the bowsprit, so I couldn't really help him. Then, a few minutes later, we heard Jeff scream. He had slipped and run the knife blade deep across the palm of his hand.

I had some experience with lacerations from my years working behind the bar, where fights, broken glass, etcetera were commonplace. We had a comprehensive first aid box on board. Jeff was bleeding profusely by the time he made it back to the cockpit. The wound was deep, but a clean cut. It possibly needed two or three stitches to pull it together. I offered to help, but Jeff just grimaced and shook his head. He wouldn't let me touch him, then went below to get a towel and said he would look after it himself. Robin and I still had to deal with the flogging headsail, so again, I made my way up to the bow.

It was still blowing hard when I reached the bowsprit. I checked out the furler, and it looked like Jeff had got the job done and managed to get the furler drum rewound again. There was so much water coming over the bow that I decided to leave it and check the fitting later, when the conditions improved. Once I made it back into the cockpit, we managed to reduce the headsail. Then, I left Robin on the helm and went below to dry off. A macabre vision greeted me as I descended the blood-smeared companionway. When I turned at the bottom of the steps, the white internal hull was covered in blood-streaked hand marks. Blood was splattered down the hull walls leading back to Jeff's cabin in the stern. There was so much blood all over the place, it looked like a murder scene, but I just couldn't feel sorry for Jeff. I was so pissed off, and I was not going to clean up Jeff's bloody mess. Sometime later, Robin cleaned it all up.

We were now only 40 nautical miles northeast of Cocos, which was just under one degree. Our final destination was the lagoon moorings at Direction Island, the northernmost island in the group of 27. The moorings were located in a horseshoe bay and were the only safe place where an international visiting yacht could anchor. Roughly 16 nautical miles north of Direction Island lay North Keeling Island, which was to the southwest ahead of us. If we sailed off the wind, we would end up many miles to the west of North Keeling Island before we could turn back south. This would mean another extra day or more on the water. So, the plan was to keep to the east as much as possible, then tack back west and at the same time stay clear of the reefs surrounding North Keeling Island, which would be close to a lee shore. Once we were clear of North Keeling, we would be in open water, and have an easy approach from the north into the moorings. Robin estimated that with a bit of luck we should arrive before midday.

COCOS. 12 DEGREES SOUTH.

Jeff didn't reappear on deck after his knife injury. Robin and I again resigned ourselves to just the two of us getting Snizort the last few miles to Cocos. Right after I came back on watch at midnight a seagull hit the mainsail, ending up dazed and flapping around on deck. Earlier, as Robin went off watch, he told me to wake him if I sighted North Keeling Island. The fallen seagull made me have an extra careful look around. As I searched the night sky along the horizon, I could just make out a thin silvery-white line of surf off to starboard. North Keeling Island! I called Robin back on deck, and he immediately spotted the surf line. "OK, JJ, start her up. Let's get out of here! We can motor sail away to give us a bit more room for our approach in the morning", but when I turned the key and pushed the start button, we just heard a loud clunk. No start!

LAND HO! COCOS KEELING AT LAST.

The engine had seized at the worst possible time. The Perkins that had been so faithful decided to die on us. Shit happens. There was nothing to do but beat into the wind and try to make it south. Then we watched together as the silver surf line grew ever closer, slowly covering more and more of the horizon to our starboard. We pushed Snizort hard, and an hour later, after several tacks, we finally slipped south of North Keeling Island and into clear water. Thankfully, the Keeling reefs were now behind us, albeit much closer than originally planned. It felt like we had done it; that the hard part was over, and now I could relax and crash for a few hours. I woke around 9am, and returned to the cockpit. Jeff was at the helm with his hand all bandaged up. There was nothing to say. The atmosphere on deck was tense, but the weather was fine. It was then I had my first sight of Cocos - a flat-topped black line of coconut trees. From our position it looked more like a massive caterpillar crawling along the horizon.

The dual ring of coral islands is less than two meters above the water at the highest point. The back of Direction Island was now just a couple of miles ahead and sheltering us from the swell. The wind eased, and we were able to sail directly into the Port Refuge channel approaches. Once we navigated through the channel, we could head to the mooring area in the lagoon. I went forward to prepare the anchor while Robin returned to the helm for our final approach. As we had no engine power, the plan was to sail into the moorings, then pull up directly into the wind and stop. At that point I would drop the anchor. We could then drift back in irons (headed into the wind) and drop the sails. Easy!

It was still blowing around 12 knots, so we charged into the moorings at 4 knots. There were several other large cruising yachts anchored around the palm-fringed lagoon, offering a fantastic view after being at sea for so long. Robin shouted for me to drop the anchor as we came up dead into the wind. I released the pawl, then the clutch on the winch and away rattled the anchor and chain. The lagoon depth at the moorings was about 5 meters. Everything was going as planned when the chain suddenly stopped with a bang. It had jammed in the hawser pipe leading up to the deck from the anchor locker, a knot in the chain somewhere. The anchor was on the bottom, but only just. We still kept moving slowly ahead, the anchor bouncing along the bottom. Then the anchor caught on something and pulled us back over onto the wind, and we started sailing, again dragging our anchor along the lagoon floor. I immediately dived below to see if I could free up the chain in the anchor locker while Robin and Jeff were trying to dump the sails. They dropped the main ok, but when they rolled in the headsail, the furler Jeff had tried to fix wound in only a few turns, then jammed up again. We still had half of the head sail out, so Snizort kept on sailing.

I didn't see what happened next, as I was below deck trying to free the tangled anchor chain, which I eventually did. The chain had only just started running free again when I heard a female's scream above as we collided with a crunch, slamming midship into a 13-meter Japanese wooden yacht called Yu Yu. The crew were on the deck, relaxing and having a drink, minding their own business, when a thirty-ton steel yacht crashed into them while they were sitting at anchor. Oh shit! What a way to arrive! Several other yachts sitting at their moorings witnessed our not-so-professional arrival. (I reckoned they were having a good laugh at us). Despite all the chaos, we had made it.

Direction Island moorings at Cocos must be one of the most visually stunning island destinations imaginable, picture postcard stuff. What a huge relief for us all! After sailing for weeks without a break, we had finally made Cocos. With the anchor now well set, Snizort slowly drifted back. We managed to get rid of the headsail and finally pulled up fifty metres astern of Yu Yu. We hurriedly launched our dinghy, attached the outboard, and then motored over to humbly apologise. Yanie, Yu Yu's skipper, was so cool. Our metal bowsprit had done a fair bit of damage to the wooden gunwale (Where the deck joins the hull), and the impact had also taken out three handrail stanchions.

Initially, we were all a bit quiet and embarrassed after climbing aboard Yu Yu. Jeff offered to pay for all the damage, but as we had a fully equipped workshop on board Snizort with lots of good hardwood timber, the logical conclusion was to fix the damage ourselves. Yanie agreed. He disappeared below deck and came back up a minute or so later with a six-pack of Budweiser beer, handed us all a cold can, and said with a big toothy smile, "Now we are all sadder, But-Wiser." That really broke the tension; we all cracked up, and everybody started laughing.

SNIZORT ALONGSIDE YU YU

I was amazed! What a guy! After smashing into his yacht and all the chaos we created, he came up with a crack like that. Absolutely brilliant!

PROBLEMS IN PARADISE

After our spectacularly embarrassing arrival, and apologies completed, we contacted the Cocos Customs so they could clear us in. They had to come from West Island, which was about 13 kms away on the other side of the lagoon. We had an hour or so to wait. Eventually, the customs boat pulled up alongside. We explained to them our engine problems and why we couldn't pick up the quarantine mooring. Dieter, the Customs Officer, was not happy with us, but understood our predicament and cleared us all in after the usual check-ups. With Customs out of the way and Snizort safely at anchor, it was time to relax and soak up the atmosphere at Cocos. We jumped back into the dinghy and headed for shore. We were all a bit unsteady when we first stepped on the coconut palm-fringed island.

As we were pulling the dinghy up the beach, a 40ft charter boat pulled up to the island jetty and unloaded a bunch of tourists. When the skipper of the boat stepped off the jetty, he looked across and recognised Robin. It was John Clunnies-Ross Jr—the owner of the Cocos Keeling Islands. Robin was an old friend of John Clunnies-Ross from his many previous visits to Cocos and had also done some personal work for the family. So, when John spotted Robin, he came over. After a friendly reunion, John invited us all to a meal at his spectacular 18th-century Victorian mansion 'Oceania House' on Home Island.

The two-story mansion was clad with white enamel-faced bricks, originally imported from Scotland to protect the home from the frequent tropical cyclonic conditions around Cocos. There was also a 2-meter-high stone wall enclosing the entire property for the same reason. The

450-strong local-Malay community lived in a village at the other end of Home Island, a narrow palm-covered strip of land, only two kilometres long and around 100 meters wide, located on the east side of the island's ringed lagoon.

As we sat dining in the chess room of a gleaming white two-story Scottish mansion on this tiny coral atoll in the middle of the Indian Ocean, I wondered how life could get much weirder. Two days ago, we were fighting the elements to stay alive, had a chaotic crash landing, and now were dining with the legendary John Clunnies-Ross. Life on the edge!

During our meal, I listened to John and learned about the history of his family and his ancestors. He was a sixth-generation descendant of the original Clunnies-Ross, a sea captain who first settled the island group around 1827. He ran the small island colony almost single-handedly until eventually importing a couple of hundred people from Malaysia and SE Asia to help establish a copra plantation business. In 1886 England took control of the strategically placed islands. Upon visiting England, Queen Victoria issued a royal decree granting Clunnies-Ross and his family the right to rule the islands in perpetuity. By making Clunnies-Ross a royal representative of the Queen, he then had total control of the island group. As time passed, he became known as the King of Cocos Islands, and his sons would continue this legacy. The family ran the islands uninterrupted for almost one hundred and fifty years until the Australian government took control in 1955.

OCEANIA HOUSE. HOME ISLAND.

For a while before our arrival on Cocos, I had been mulling over telling Jeff I'd had enough and wanted out. I couldn't see myself putting up with another two or three weeks of Jeff's BS. First, I thought it would be a good idea to have a conversation with Robin. He understood how I felt but, at the same time, pointed out that I should at least stay until Jeff could find a replacement for me. Where? He could also demand that the airfare and his costs be repaid. Additionally, booking a one-way ticket from Cocos back to Australia was over $1,000 US, which I didn't have. Win or lose, I decide to see the whole thing out and put up with Jeff and his mood swings for another couple of weeks. It was just another job at the end of the day, and who knows, we still might get paid.

Snizort had multiple problems that needed attention beyond the new parts for the autopilot. We managed to locate the local marine mechanic, Mr Abidin, a Malay guy from the village. After checking out the Perkins he told us we had a serious problem. Seawater was in the cylinder head! The only way seawater could have got into the cylinder head is through the exhaust pipe at the stern. So, after figuring out what was needed, Jeff, who had reverted to the pleasant, cool-in-charge captain, ordered new parts to be flown in from mainland Australia. There was only one flight a week from Perth, a milk run north through Indonesia and Christmas Island to Cocos, the last stop.

No one told us, but a new casino was being constructed on Christmas Island at the time. This was also an Australian-controlled Island about 900 kilometres east of Cocos and much closer to the Sumatran coast. All air freight coming to Cocos had to be booked on a priority-paid basis, as there was a high demand for air freight. Bad luck for us! Our parts were only booked as standard air freight. The plane was full of priority-paid cargo, mainly for the new casino on Christmas Island. So, our parts never even made it on board. After waiting a week for parts that didn't arrive, Jeff discovered that priority paid was the only way we would get anything on to the plane. He had to book again, and I think that's when he remembered to get the EPIRB. (Emergency Position Indicating Radio Beacon).

EPIRB technology was still new to the yachting world at that time and was initially not considered essential to have onboard. Ironic that the engine breakdown was actually what saved our lives. But we didn't know it then. When we left Langkawi, I don't recall ever seeing an EPIRB on board Snizort. They are usually kept on a bracket in a handy place to grab around the cockpit in an emergency. Jeff only decided to fly up the new EPIRB after our engine failure off Cocos, which meant we had to wait for another week. It was not all bad. I spent a few days getting to know the crew on Yu Yu while helping repair the damage to their boat after our collision. The all-Japanese crew consisted of one female and three guys. Yanie, the Captain, his very attractive partner Sargo, Tony, and Yamarta, the crew's youngest member. He looked around 25 years old.

THE *CREW ON YU YU. YANIE, SARGO, TONY, YAMARTA.*

I felt quite envious as they all seemed to get on great together. Yamarta said he was a keen diver but was not very experienced. I told him he was in for a treat. For the next few days, after working on the damage to Yu Yu, we free dived together on some of the world's most spectacular and pristine coral reefs. I soon discovered that Yamarta's previous diving experience mainly consisted of just floating face down. Initially, he watched me for a while from the surface and then, with a bit of help, quickly got the hang of hyperventilating. After that, I couldn't slow him down - he was a natural. There was a breakthrough in the outer ring of reefs at the east end of Direction Island that flowed continuously into the lagoon. It was a short walk out to the end of a horseshoe-shaped beach, maybe two hundred meters before diving in. Even if all you can do is float face down with a snorkel, the marine life and coral concentration was fantastic in the warm, crystal-clear water. A golden, sandy bottom awaits you once through the natural gap, around 30 meters long and 3 meters wide. Then there are several steel posts driven into the sand with a hand chain running along the top so you can pull yourself safely back to the beach and avoid getting swept into the centre of the lagoon. Free diving for the beginner doesn't get much better anywhere in the world than the Cocos Islands.

FUGU

Yanie, the skipper, was a very likeable guy. When he told me he had previously owned a nightclub in Osaka, we discovered we shared a similar history, and given that he was around the same vintage as me, we hit it off like a house on fire. Yamarta, the youngest crew member, was the son of his close friend, who owned a fish factory. I was under the impression that when the voyage was over, Yamarta was expected to take over the family business from his dad. Yanie also made a beautiful comment about his partner, Sargo. He said, "Sargo is like the oil on the water when the crew disagrees" She had a very serene presence. Tony, the other crew member, was around 40, easy going, and a carpenter... very handy to have on a wooden yacht.

The fish Yamarta and I speared was prepared in authentic Japanese style by the crew on Yu Yu. I asked Yanie if the fish he was preparing was a sushi dish. He shook his head, gave me his big toothy smile, and then told me that this dish is known as Ikizukuri, prepared and eaten while the flesh is still alive and shimmering. He dipped a piece in a dressing and handed it to me. It melted in my mouth. Indeed, a rare dish that few can enjoy - what a privilege. Then another day, Yanie hooked a big toadfish, (we call them blow fish in Oz). I said, "You can't eat that, those fish are very poisonous. "Oh yes" replied Yanie "This preparation is called Fugu, only the internal organs and the blood is poison. You will see when I fillet the fish, JJ. I will cut not too close to the skeleton." So I thought, "Well, he seems to know what he's talking about and very confident, if I go, we all go.' The loose skin was removed, and the flesh was washed. Then, large fillets were cut into smaller pieces, grilled, and placed on lettuce leaves with rice, accompanied by a dressing. Delicious white flesh, and we all lived to tell the tale.

As I had so much time on my hands, I made friends with Dieter, the Customs Officer, and volunteered to help out with customs when new boats arrived, guiding them into the moorings by radio. The days slipped by. Parties on yachts and BBQs on the beach at night, lots of drinking, fishing, and messing around in boats. Island life at its very best. Hard to take!

Our parts finally arrived, and all the other work that needed to be done on Snizort was finished, but we still had one big problem. Our Perkins main engine was dead, getting seawater in the cylinder head had caused significant internal damage, and it would be impossible to repair on Cocos. A full strip-down and rebuild were needed if the Perkins was ever going to run again. Robin suggested getting towed out to sea and then sailing back to Fremantle. 2000 miles with no main engine, just the Honda generator and the solar panels for power. We would probably need a tow-in at the other end. I was not happy with the idea of just relying on the wind. I knew not having a main engine could easily add another week at sea to our voyage, but it seemed we were stuck and had run out of options.

TOWED OUT

Getting Snizort ready for the next leg of our journey was intense. We were taking a calculated risk, 2000 nautical miles with only our sails for drive. Then, it was time to say goodbye to the crew of Yu Yu. I asked Yanie out of curiosity, "What does the name of your boat mean?" "Play together," was the answer. They left a couple of days before us on the 23rd. The next stop for them was the Maldives, 1500 miles due west. It should have been an easy passage with the trades behind them all the way. (Yamarta kept in touch with me by snail mail for months afterwards from destinations all over the globe).

Then, it was our turn to leave. Jeff organized a tow out of the moorings for 1500 hours, a fresh sea breeze to accompany us as we left Direction Island. The tow line was dropped at 3:30 pm. A wave goodbye to the tow boat crew, and we were on our way. Predictably, the trades were blowing from the southeast, precisely the direction that we needed to go. The direct heading to Fremantle from Cocos was 160 degrees SSE. The best course we could make was approximately 210 degrees SSW, about 45 degrees off the wind. So, we were heading out into the middle of the Indian Ocean toward Mauritius, which meant we would be sailing away from the West Australian coast until we could get far enough south to pick up the prevailing south-westerly systems. They would give us the right sailing conditions for heading east and back to the Australian mainland. It looked like we were in for a long haul. Still, after our extended break on Cocos, we were refreshed and happy to be heading home. Jeff was in a good mood; Robin was on the chart table, and I was more than ready for the voyage. Finally, we were on our way. Fremantle was the next stop.

The Cocos Island group comprises a double ring of 27 islands atop twin extinct volcano craters, a very steep drop-off into thousands of feet of water on all sides. Huge shoals of fish were swimming continuously around the outer reefs. I had set up the fishing gear on the back of Snizort after we left the moorings. Only minutes after we dropped the tow rope, I picked up a nice, big Barracuda, a great start. Then, as Cocos quickly disappeared over the horizon, I spent the next couple of hours below deck trying to find all the annoying things that rattle and bang on a boat at sea.

WATER IN THE BILGES

As night fell, the wind and swell picked up. Snizort was close-hauled with reefed sails, thumping through the rising sea. I was due on the dog watch again, so after our evening meal I tried to get some sleep. At 3.45am Robin woke me with a coffee. "Morning, JJ, time to go." Overnight, the weather had deteriorated, and the swell had built up to around 4 meters. Robin finished the log and left me with the rest of my watch. It takes a while to get it together at that time of the morning when the sea and sky look black. Low cloud cover means no stars or visual horizon, steering solely by the compass with only the dim red glow from the compass dome for company. Eventually, I settled into the rhythm of the sea. Four hours of helming hard on the wind.

Around 5 am, an hour or so before daylight, Jeff appeared on deck and said he had woken up to take a piss and could hear water sloshing around. Then he went back below deck to check the bilges again. (They were dry when I came on watch at 4 a.m.) When he returned to the cockpit a few minutes later, he looked pretty distraught and announced, "There's quite a lot of water. We've got a bad leak somewhere!" I immediately thought that a skin fitting had ruptured (fittings and valves that go through the hull wall). Jeff went below again to wake up Robin. I thought Robin was going to be really pissed off since he had only been off-watch for about 2 hours. Initially, I was not overly concerned. I thought that, as I was still on watch, they would find the source of the leak, plug or seal it off, and that would resolve the problem in time for breakfast. Maybe 5 minutes went by, and then Jeff came up again, anxiety written on his face, and said, "We can't find the leak anywhere, and I think it's getting much worse. Go and have a look for yourself."

I had been having problems with the helm just before Jeff arrived. Something felt wrong with the steering. Jeff took over the helm, and I went below for a look. Whoa! I was more than a little surprised to see water starting to splash up through the plywood flooring. Not good! I looked across the saloon. Robin had his head buried in the back of a locker. As he stood up and turned, I said, "Now what?" Robin still didn't seem too worried. He said, "We've checked all the skin fittings, and they are okay. The water in the bilges is seawater, so we haven't split a freshwater tank. It's unlikely, but maybe the leak is coming in through the exhaust pipe we sealed before we left Cocos." (The exhaust ran through the hull and under the floor in Jeff's master cabin and then out through the transom at the stern.)

We called Jeff back down below. He locked the helm, and then we all went aft into his cabin together. There was a raised queen-sized bed in the middle of the floor. The mattress and bedding were pulled to one side, revealing an insulated plywood panel on top. We removed all the top of the bed and the insulation. Below that was the steering gear, a big metal frame with hydraulic arms, the rudder post in the middle, running down into a bearing fitted through the hull. Next, we located the insulated exhaust pipe under the floor on the starboard side. Before we left Cocos, the exhaust pipe had been tightly sealed off as the Perkins was dead. Then we carefully inspected the entire length of the exhaust system, from the back of the engine to where it exits the transom, but no leaks were found anywhere.

HULL SPLITTING OPEN

Where else was there to look? By this time, the water was around 100 mm deep in the bilges under the bed, sloshing around the base of the steering gear. Snizort was riding up one swell and down the next. As the bow rose, a rush of cold seawater flooded back into Jeff's cabin, all around our feet, and then our attention was suddenly riveted. We were all transfixed. A thin, brilliant blue - white light shone up through the black water under the steering gear. Suddenly, the split appeared to open right up. The hull was splitting open forward of the rudder post bearing, and the split seemed to be running along a welding seam. The blue - white light shining up from the sea below appeared to be about half a meter long. Sea water was visibly bubbling in under pressure as the split in the hull opened wider. Then, as suddenly as it appeared, the light seemed to switch off. We thought Snizort must be twisting in the swell and splitting open.

There was another very serious problem. The battery compartment, which was located under the saloon floor, had flooded. So, the bilge pump had lost power. We had a manual bilge pump in the saloon on the side of the console next to the central steering station, but it was a whale-type pump. This type of pump is designed to push water up a pipe, not suck the water up a long way. The pump had been installed nearly a meter and a half above the bilges. We tried pumping, but it was never going to work until it was close to being submerged. There was absolutely no way of getting rid of so much water continuously flooding into the hull.

We couldn't even send a Mayday without the batteries. (I thought later that it would have been a good idea to carry a small 12-volt motorcycle battery for just such an emergency). I made my way back to the helm while Robin and Jeff tried to figure out what to do next. We were drifting side onto the sea, rolling, and lurching in the swell. Once back in the cockpit, I grabbed the helm to try to get us back on the wind, but there was no response. Then the wheel seemed momentarily to free up, only to lock again moments later. We were drifting dead in the water. Jeff came back up on deck. When I told him that the steering gear also seemed to be jammed, he started shaking his head over and over. At that time, I recall looking at my watch, and it was already 9am.

Robin came up from below and said, "We are sinking in slow motion!" Think! Think! What if I went over the side with a towel smeared with thick grease and jammed the towel into the split with a screwdriver? Maybe the water pressure would keep the towel pressed against the break in the hull, and the greasy towel would help seal the split, hopefully giving us some more time. My idea probably wouldn't have worked, but since nobody came up with any better suggestions, Robin prepared our rope ladder on the leeward side, away from the wind, near the stern. I stripped down and just had my dive mask on, a safety rope tied around me. Robin was holding the other end. Getting the two meters down the rope ladder with Snizort jumping about wasn't easy. I kept swinging out and then slamming back in against the hull wall. When I finally reached the bottom of the ladder and was half-submerged, I leaned over and stuck my head underwater for a quick look. The problem was immediately obvious. I remember thinking, 'Oh, no!' The spade rudder appeared to have broken free around the bearing. From my position on the bottom of the rope ladder I could see it hanging under the stern, swinging around and twisting at the steel hull. It was just a matter of time before Snizort split wide open.

There was no point in even trying to swim down and get to the break in the hull now. At the same time, Snizort was nose-diving in the swell. Then, as she lifted, all the water inside the hull rushed back to the stern again. The hull slammed back down hard right next to my head. It was really too dangerous for me to even try. I made my way up the rope ladder and climbed back onto the deck. Jeff was looking at me intently when I faced him, and then I gave him the bad news. "It looks to me like the rudder bearing has broken free from the hull, and the rudder is just swinging around like a pendulum. That is what's splitting us open! Unless we can come up with another plan, I think we're going down!" Jeff slowly shook his head. Robin looked on but had nothing to add.

ABANDON SHIP

Above deck, things seemed normal, but below deck it was chaos. Tons of water were rushing around, blowing the cupboards open. Bedding, bottles, floorboards - anything that floated – was sloshing everywhere. As I tried to absorb the pandemonium around me, I experienced the odd feeling of being detached. I went into slow-motion state and just kept moving, trying not to think too far ahead. We didn't even have a regulation emergency inflatable rubber life raft, just our 3-meter Stacer aluminium dinghy. It wouldn't sink as the bench seats were full of foam, but that was little consolation in the circumstances. First, we had to get the dinghy untied from the davits on Snizort's stern, then launched and secured alongside with a long mooring line. Once in the water, the dinghy was jumping around and bouncing off Snizort's hull, so Jeff climbed down into the dinghy and tried to put in a fender and hold off. I climbed down and helped Jeff secure the outboard to the transom of the dinghy, and then climbed back up and onto the deck. Robin went below again to retrieve some more gear and the binoculars. Suddenly, it hit me. I felt a wave of panic. I thought, 'this is crazy, but it's really happening! We're all going to get off Snizort into this tiny aluminium dinghy in the middle of the Indian Ocean!' I could feel my heart thumping in my chest.

Jeff stayed down in the dinghy. The two 20-litre freshwater containers we had tied on deck and another 20-litre container that I had filled with petrol for the outboard were lowered down next. The rocket flares and safety gear were put into a grab bag. We had a bucket and several ice cream containers for bailing out. I had previously made some crude oars for the dinghy, so we bought them along as well. Food was next. There were heaps of cans below, but it was getting impossible down there. Stuff was flying about all over the place, but somehow we managed to retrieve a sack full of tinned food, another pack of plastic 1-litre water bottles, and a very wet box of chocolate bars. Snizort was now sitting nose down in the sea, no more tipping back and forth with the swell. It was hard to guess how long she would stay afloat, and we didn't want to risk being on board or tied up alongside if she suddenly started to go down. Lastly, we put our heavy-duty sailing gear on and then our life jackets over the top.

ANOTHER DISASTER

The problem was, what to take? I put my camera, wallet, and diary into a waterproof grab bag. My Swiss army knife in a pocket, along with my sunnies. Next, I put my dive mask in another plastic bag with a pair of jeans and another jacket - not very logical when I think back now. I also kept a pair of Nike runners that I had bought just before we left Langkawi. Robin was doing final checks and still getting things together. When I looked over the side, Jeff was down in the dinghy waiting for us and fending off from Snizort's hull. I suppose he figured there was no point in coming back on board. We passed our gear down to him.

When I told Robin that Jeff was waiting for us in the dinghy, he stopped momentarily, looked up at me from the cockpit hatch, and said, "Keep him busy. Give him the EPIRB." I picked up the beacon and leaned over the safety line. Jeff stood up and reached for the EPIRB as I handed it to him. While standing in the dinghy with the beacon in one hand, he pulled out the chrome telescopic aerial with the other hand, then lost his balance and fell backwards into the stern of the dinghy. When he sat up moments later, the EPIRB was in one hand, but the aerial was in the other, snapped clean off at the base.

Oh fuck! I couldn't believe what I was seeing! Just when I thought things couldn't get any worse, this happened. I knew we were literally dead without the EPIRB. Jeff sat with his head down, then slowly looked up at me. He had that look of total despair in his eyes and just kept shaking his head slowly. I went back and gave Robin the bad news. He stopped momentarily, then reached into his grab bag, pulled out a pair of pliers, handed them to me and said, "All we can do is crunch the bottom of the aerial, push it back into the base and hope for the best. Tell Jeff to keep the EPIRB inboard and turn it on, and don't let the ariel touch the hull."

Robin's unflappable confidence gave me strength. I calmed down, then took a couple of deep breaths and tried to think logically. Just face one problem at a time: Panic achieves nothing. Try and stay positive. We're not dead yet!

I handed the pliers down to Jeff. He crunched up the base of the aerial and then pushed it back into the main body of the EPIRB. Jeff turned the beacon on, looked up, and gave me a thumbs up. The rest of our gear, along with the food and water bottles, was lowered down next. Then it was my turn. I had a feeling of dread as I clambered over the side for the last time and down that rope ladder - like facing your execution. Robin followed a few minutes later.

Finally, we were all aboard our 3-meter rescue vessel. Jeff and I sat on the middle bench facing the bow, with Robin in the stern sitting next to the outboard, each of us clipped on with a safety line. We were still moored alongside Snizort, bouncing off the steel hull, giving us some shelter from the 15-knot trade winds. Then we all stopped whatever we were doing and looked at each other. No one had said much while we were abandoning Snizort. I think we had been trying to avoid eye contact. Everyone had just been getting on with the next bit in a sort of robotic fashion, maybe not wanting to show any fear. But this was now our inescapable reality. On one side of our bouncing dinghy loomed the wall of Snizort's listing hull, and on the other, the endless void of the Indian Ocean.

It took us a few minutes to take stock and assess our situation. The three of us, along with all our gear, food supplies, water containers, the outboard motor, and the fuel container, left our dinghy with only a few inches of freeboard. We all agreed to dump everything that wasn't absolutely necessary. Losing as much weight as possible was crucial before we cast off from the shelter of Snizort's hull. One wave could easily swamp us. Why we bought all the unnecessary clothing, I don't know. Robin had a leather jacket and some clothing in his bag. Jeff only had a small bag and a few personal items. I dumped my jeans, jacket, and the new Nikes over the side. Jeff noticed that I had kept my dive mask and the 35mm Minolta. Then he made a sarcastic remark, "A photo opportunity, or maybe you're going for a dive." I said nothing, but thought that the dive mask didn't really weigh anything, and it might just come in handy. I thought about dumping the Minolta, but I just wasn't ready to give it up yet. That left us with just our sailing gear and the life jackets we were wearing. Still, getting rid of our gear didn't make that much difference to the freeboard. If we had pushed off then, I don't think we would have lasted more than a few minutes in the open sea before we were swamped.

THE SEA ANCHOR

Robin came up with a plan that I am sure ultimately saved our lives. Because they are less dense, fresh water and petrol float in seawater. We tied the petrol container and one of the freshwater containers to the end of our long mooring rope. The other end was then secured to the tow hitch on the bow post of our dinghy with a shackle. The result was another couple of inches of freeboard. The

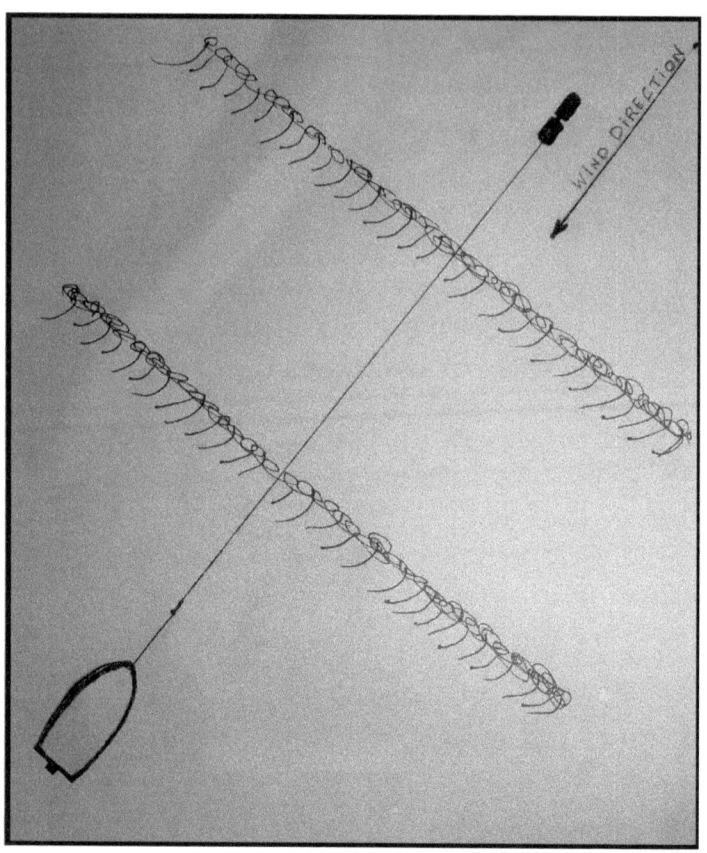

ROBIN'S SEA ANCHOR

polyethene fuel and water containers floated about 20 meters away on the surface, acting as a sea anchor and keeping our bow facing into the ocean swell and waves. Once we had the sea anchor system fully rigged, I gingerly pushed off from Snizort's hull with one of my homemade oars, and just for a little extra lousy luck, the blade of my oar snapped in half. I was about to throw it away in disgust when Robin said, "No, we still might need it JJ. Half an oar is better than no oar."

We slowly drifted away from Snizort. She was clearly down by her bow. There was a brief period of calm, and then, once clear of the shelter Snizort's hull provided, the open sea and wind hit us hard. Initially, the sea anchor wasn't particularly tight, and it looked for a moment as though we might get side-on to the sea, which would have been a disaster.

SNIZORT DRIFTS AWAY ABANDONED

Thankfully, the bow suddenly jerked around to face the ocean swell and waves head-on as the slack in the sea anchor line stretched tight. Bailing out almost continuously was not going to be an option if we were to stay afloat with the sea anchor constantly dragging the bow around. During those first few minutes, as we drifted away from Snizort, I felt an overwhelming sense of hopelessness. This was suicide. We really didn't have a chance. It's just a matter of time before we were swamped or flipped by a big wave, maybe an hour or maybe a day before the inevitable.

While these thoughts were running around my head, I didn't notice what Jeff was doing sitting next to me, and seemingly out of nowhere, he suddenly produced a bottle of rum and drinking glasses. Incredible! A last drink to Snizort. Jeff handed us each a glass. No speeches or anything like that. I don't think anything was said. I took the glass and swallowed it all down in a couple of shots. Despite all the evidence I have read to the contrary about drinking at times like this, at that moment, after hours and hours of extreme pressure, when the first mouthful of rum slid down my throat, it sent a beautiful warm glow racing around inside me. For the first time that day I felt re-energized. I just had one glass. Jeff and Robin finished off the rest of the bottle together, but I didn't want to get drunk at a time like this. No, that would have felt like giving up to me. Then I decided, what the hell, this was indeed a photo opportunity. I picked up the Minolta and took several pics of Snizort as she drifted away. Also, as can be seen below, there is a shot of us having a last drink to her. While I was taking the pics, my thinking was that even if we all died, there was a slim chance that someone might find my photographic record of our final journey together.

A LAST DRINK TO SNIZORT

We were drifting backwards in a north-westerly direction with our bow kept up to the waves by the drag from the sea anchor. Robin estimated that Cocos was around 100 nautical miles away to the northeast of our position. We were drifting further and further from the Australian mainland and Cocos Islands, carried by the Northeast Trade Winds. There was no possibility of using the outboard for that distance in these conditions with only 20 litres of fuel. We thought about ditching the outboard. Losing around 40 kilos would give us more desperately needed freeboard, but the outboard could still be a lifesaver for us, so we decided to keep it. The EPIRB was sitting next to us, pushed in between the plastic water bottles with its broken, wobbly aerial. I picked it up and read in the instructions that the battery life was 40 hours. I thought about the time the EPIRB had already been on for and said to Robin, "Do you think we should conserve the battery and turn off the EPIRB once it gets dark? Then we would still have hours of run time tomorrow. Nobody's going to come for us at night anyway." Robin agreed. Jeff nodded but made no comment

Now, there was just the sound of the wind and waves constantly slapping against the aluminium hull. Jeff was sitting next to me with his head down, bailing out. I turned around. Robin was sitting in the stern, next to the outboard, blankly staring out across the sea. There was nothing left to say. Negative stuff started flooding into my head. The last couple of years had all gone wrong. The loss of my business, the never-ending litigation, and my partner giving up on me. Why? I felt like a total loser. All my good luck had been used up, and now it ends like this? I am going to die out here in the middle of nowhere. We were not expected back in Aussie for at least two or three weeks, so I guessed we would be long dead before anyone raised the alarm. No one would miss us. We would probably get a mention on the evening news. "The yacht

Snizort and crew were missing at sea!" Robin suddenly broke up my gloomy thoughts. "JJ, do you have your Swiss Army knife handy?"

Robin's latest idea was to remove the 50mm mooring rope attached around the gunnel (top edge of the dinghy's hull). This rope acted as a fender and ran around our little boat. It was also very wet and heavy! A strong nylon cord was stitched around the rope and through small holes that had been drilled through the hull of the dinghy. Robin said, "Let's cut the cord off the fender, and then we can dump the heavy rope. That should make us just a bit lighter." I agreed immediately. "Let's do it!"

Then Jeff turned to me and said these words I will never forget: "Why are you both kidding yourselves? You know we're all going to die." No one said anything for a while. I didn't reply, but I thought, 'Well, you're probably right,' but I didn't need that pushed in my face just when I was trying to think more positively. Anyway, getting rid of the heavy rope was something to do, to occupy my brain and pass some time. Robin and I got into it. Awkwardly moving around the dinghy in our heavy-duty sailing gear with life jackets over the top was a real balancing act. I lost my grip a couple of times and ended up rolling around the floor when our sea anchor snapped tight, but 30 minutes later we had cut the fender rope free. Once we got rid of the weight of the heavy fender rope, the improvement to our freeboard was immediate.

Robin suggested that instead of simply losing the 50-mm polypropylene rope, we should separate the strands and add them to our sea anchor. I said, "Yes, okay, let's do it, anything that helps." That took up a bit more of the day and went well, but at the same time, we had created another problem. Our Stacer dinghy now had 30 or more small 6ml drill holes just beneath the top edge of the aluminium hull, where the fender rope ties originally passed through. Now, when waves hit us, water squirted through in little jets all over the place. Jeff was shaking his head again, but he didn't say anything this time. Robin immediately bent down and pulled his size 12 rubber thongs off his feet. "OK, JJ, just use your knife to cut rubber plugs from my thongs, and then we can bung up all the holes." Another half hour or so passed, and we were done. The heavy-duty fender rope was gone, and we were not exactly what you might call watertight, but now we were sitting a little higher out of the water. The fuel and freshwater containers at the end of our sea anchor were doing a great job of keeping the bow up to the wind and waves. All this work had considerably reduced the amount of water coming over the side, so Robin suggested a watch rotation with just one bailing, giving us each an individual break from the continuous need to bail out. At least now it felt like we had a more realistic chance of staying alive, even if it was only for a little while longer. That's all that really counted in the end - more time!

We watched all afternoon as Snizort slowly drifted further and further until she was a couple of miles away from our position. At the same time, her stern was gradually rising higher and higher out of the ocean as the bow slowly sank deeper into the sea. Around 1700 hours her stern went vertical and she slipped below the waves. I took a few pics as she was going down. Not too clear from that distance. The three of us all looked on in silence as the sun sank lower into the now-empty horizon. While Snizort was afloat, there was a feeling that we were somehow still connected to the world outside. Now she was gone an overwhelming realisation hit us. We were truly alone. There was a minute or two of silence. Robin said something, but I wasn't really listening. I remembered my little black pocket diary and decided to try and put something down on paper.

SNIZORT GOING DOWN

26th JUNE DIARY ENTRY

"Well, I'm in the middle of the Indian Ocean with Robin and Jeff. Snizort sank at 5 pm. We are in the dinghy, hoping to God the EPIRB still works, a crazy day. Rudder broke free and tore a hole in the hull, rough as guts. Abandoned Snizort 11.30 am."

Moments later, while I was bent over trying to write, a wave slapped the side of the dinghy and washed over me and the diary, leaving me with a lot of damp, blurred pages. That was the only entry I made while we were in the dinghy. Daylight was nearly gone, and none of us had eaten all day. I hadn't felt any sensation of hunger, but we all ate a can of tinned something or other and a chocolate bar. Each of us had our own 1 litre plastic water bottle. Then, we watched together in silence as the sun slowly sank below a grey horizon. I guess we all had the same inevitable thought, 'Is this going to be my last sunset?'

We were all clipped into the dinghy with our safety lines. If a wave did roll us over during the night, would we get entangled or trapped underneath? Different scenarios ran through my head. I only weighed around 70 kilos, so I figured I could pull myself back into the dinghy without a problem, but Robin would have weighed over 130 kilos in the water with his wet weather gear on. Being so heavy, if he had attempted to get back into a half-swamped dinghy, I'm sure he would have just rolled us right over again. Then what? Hanging onto the side of our little boat at night in the middle of the Indian Ocean for how long? I doubted if Jeff would survive that sort of situation. He hadn't said anything for quite a while. It seemed to me he had already resigned himself to his fate.

THE LIGHT

Jeff was head down, half asleep next to me, both of us rolling around on the bench seat. It was 7 pm. The sea looked black all around us, glittering with phosphorescence atop the waves. Aside from the stars and some cloud cover, the sky appeared just as black as the sea. I found it nearly impossible to relax with so much movement going on. I felt tense, just waiting for something else to happen or go wrong, coupled with the noise from the aluminium hull getting slapped around by the wind and waves.

Then, right on the horizon, I noticed a glint of light. We were drifting backwards, sliding up and down 3-meter swells topped with boiling white water, so our vision was restricted to just a few seconds on the wave crests, but there it was again. I turned around and asked Robin if he could see the light. Then Jeff woke up, and now we could all see the light. Action stations! In the grab bag with the flares, we had two Dolphin waterproof torches. The plan was that I would stand up on the middle bench seat of the dinghy, Robin and Jeff holding my legs, helping me to balance. I unhooked my safety line. Just trying to stand upright on the bench seat with the dinghy jumping about and two guys struggling to hold on to your legs is best left to your imagination, but somehow they got me upright. Once I was standing, I just tried to focus all my attention on the light. I held the dolphin torch as high as I could above my head, pointed it at the light, and then started to flash out an S.O.S signal. But we slid down to the bottom of the next swell, so I had to wait until we were high enough again to see the light. While I was signalling, the light got noticeably brighter, and then the light started to spread along the horizon. Oh no! I instantly realised it was simply the moon rising. I looked down and said, "It's just the moon."

No jokes, no one said a word as they helped me sit down again, nothing more to say. Silence. I clipped myself in again and gave the torch back to Robin. The disappointment was crushing. I sat staring blankly into the sea. There wouldn't be any amazing rescue story tonight.

Hours slipped by. While rolling around in my seat, I started to recall a story my dad had told me when I was a boy. I was named after his brother, John Jack who was part of the crew on a ship that was torpedoed during the Second World War.

WORLD WAR TWO

The second thread of my story begins here. I wish there was more I could say about the life of the man I was named after. I don't recall my father ever saying much about his family in Scotland after we immigrated to Australia, only that there were four brothers. The youngest was John Jack. Dad said his brothers called him Jack. This was not a lot for me to go on. At one point I did a little digging into the family archives, with little success. Years would pass before I unearthed the rest of the story in South Africa from Uncle Bill, Dad's older brother.

DAD'S SILVER SPOON SET

The phrase 'Born with a silver spoon in his mouth' applied to the four brothers born into a wealthy family. Well-heeled parents would traditionally give each child an engraved silver set at the time of their christening. Grandad, another J.J. Paterson, was referred to as a land agent and alcohol merchant. They lived in an impressive family home on the banks of the River Clyde close to Glasgow. However, this privileged lifestyle came to an end for the brothers with the onset of the First World War, followed by the depression, and then the Second World War. Times were tough. All the money was gone.

Jack became a marine engineer in his adult life. Like thousands of young men, Jack wanted to do his bit for the war effort, but not everyone could go and fight, so as an officer in the merchant navy, Jack decided to join the North Atlantic convoys. His older brother Bill was a foreman ganger on the Liverpool wharf - the sort of guy with contacts who could get you a job. When Jack applied for a second engineer officer position, it was his brother Bill who arranged for his maiden Atlantic crossing on board the SS Cerinthus.

The Cerinthus was a 4000-ton tanker with a maximum speed of 10 knots. The Cerinthus left Liverpool on 25th October, 1942, sailing in ballast (no cargo) bound for the coast of West Africa. They stayed with the North Atlantic convoy of 59 ships and destroyer escorts for the first week. Then, on the 2nd of November, the Cerinthus left the shelter of the convoy and turned south. They were heading for their next port of call to pick up cargo in Freetown on the West African coast, but now they were alone and unescorted.

All went well until the 10th of November around midnight. Off the coast of West Africa at a position 12 degrees 47min N, a location southwest of the Cape Verde islands, they were intercepted and torpedoed by German U-boat U128. The first torpedo hit amidships. Luckily, there was no major explosion as they were carrying water ballast, but several of the crew were killed. The remainder managed to escape in the ship's two lifeboats. U128 fired two more torpedoes. One hit around the engine room, and the other missed. Cerinthus stayed afloat. According to U-boat Captain Ulrich Heyse (Iron Cross), U128 surfaced at daylight. The Cerinthus was then hit with 70 rounds from their deck gun. Finally, she succumbed to the shelling, rolled over, and sank.

The U-boat captain then commenced to search for survivors, but reported finding none. The surviving crew of the Cerinthus had all abandoned ship earlier and escaped under the cover of night after the first torpedo hit. The two lifeboats managed to stay together for several days, but then a violent storm separated them. One lifeboat contained 15 survivors, including the chief officer.

The other boat had Captain James Chadwick and another 19 men, including my Uncle John Jack. On December 1st, a Sunderland flying boat spotted the chief officers' lifeboat, and hours later, they were rescued by HMS Bridgewater. All were saved after 22 days adrift - very lucky!

Unfortunately, luck tragically abandoned the other lifeboat. For two horrendous months, the men drifted over 700 miles west, slowly dying one by one from lack of water and exposure. No one can possibly imagine what hardships they went through. No words are adequate to describe or put into print their ordeal. Finally, after 77 days adrift, on 24 January, 1943, a US naval vessel, the SS Kentuckian, at a position 11` 22 Nth, found Captain James Chadwick's lifeboat drifting with one sole survivor, William Colbourn. Six other bodies were in the boat with him, one of them second engineer officer John Jack Paterson: deceased 9th January, 1943, age 28.

William Colbourn, after his rescue by the Kentuckian, was in a shocking state, both mentally and physically. My uncle Bill said that it wasn't mentioned in the official report, but there were also signs of cannibalism among the dead. Colbourn was put ashore in Port of Spain, Trinidad, on 31 January 1943. Eventually, he was repatriated to the UK, where he was then placed in permanent sanatorium care. During World War 2, Uncle Bill said they would say, 'He's gone Doolally' - an expression I hadn't heard before. I later discovered that Doolally was a World War II British Army transit camp in western India. Men would spend time there after suffering from shell shock, now more palatably called post-traumatic stress disorder. The British Army command didn't want the general public to see the men so severely traumatised in that state, so they disappeared, kept in Doolally, some for the rest of their lives. Many of them were classified as permanently mentally insane.

ENDLESS NIGHT

Back in our 3-meter lifeboat, all those thoughts were running around in my head. Of course, I only knew the broad outline of the story from my childhood. It just didn't seem possible; there I was, exactly 50 years later and in pretty much the same situation as my Uncle Jack, the man I was named after.

Time felt like it had been stretched like a piece of chewing gum. I had been awake since 3.30 am. The words of a song I had heard long before started running around in my head, 'When the waves turn the minutes to hours.' At some point, I must have fallen asleep sitting up next to Jeff, both of us rolling around and constantly bumping into each other. I remember dreaming, and my dream was about our situation. Somebody said something, but I wasn't sure if I was still dreaming or if I was awake. I could hear Robin behind me scraping with his bailer on the hull and the constant noise of the wind and sea. Nothing seemed real. The whole night went like that. Sitting. Nodding. Fading in and out. Half-awake in a nightmare world until cold seawater hit my face. Start bailing, then drift off again. When daylight finally came, I was stiff and aching all over, but at the same time surprised that we were still alive. Somehow, we had made it through the night without being swamped. Robin turned the EPIRB back on. The sea was now calmer but still with a 3-meter swell, so we could take a break from the constant need to bail out. We were bobbing around like a cork on the end of the sea anchor. Our bow constantly rose to the oncoming waves, the occasional whitecap breaking over the bow into our little lifeboat. Morning and it was time to eat and pass out another litre bottle of water each. We had been sitting upright for over 20 hours. Trying to move around meant untying our safety lines - no point! I looked at Jeff's face and hair, then around at Robin. I thought it was ironic. All the dried and crusted salt spray made us look like we had been sprinkled with ice.

THE WAVE

Sometime around mid-morning, I heard a roaring noise. I looked up just in time to see a wall of white water bearing down on us. Someone yelled out, "Hang on", as the bow of our dinghy rose up and then disappeared into the breaking wave. It swept right over us. Lots of sea foam but the wave didn't totally swamp us. We went up and over the top, all drenched and thrown around a bit, but amazingly our dinghy didn't capsize. (Our faithful sea anchor had done its job again.) When we recovered and sorted ourselves out, our boat had taken a fair bit of water.

We were busy bailing out as fast as we could when Jeff discovered that the EPRIB was now lying underwater at the bottom of the hull amongst the plastic drink bottles, and the chrome telescopic aerial was missing. After a short search, we found it under the middle seat. The aerial had pulled out of the base again and was now badly kinked in the middle. Jeff picked it up carefully, slowly shaking his head. "Sometimes it's hard to stay positive! Should we try and straighten out the kink in the aerial or not?" It looked so fragile and could easily snap in half. That would have been another disaster, so we decided to leave it, bent as it was. Jeff and Robin got together and crimped the bottom of the ariel with the pliers for a second time, then pushed it back into the damaged base of the EIPRB. This was the second time the aerial had pulled out, so when the bottom of the ariel was crimped again, it had become too small for the hole in the base. We now couldn't get a good tight fit around the bottom of the ariel. Jeff tried to squeeze the broken ends together with the pliers. Then Robin suggested finding a safe place for the EIPRB. I watched on, thinking, 'Like where?' Our efforts looked so pathetic. It seemed a total waste of time with everything soaked in seawater and the aerial all loose and bent, but what else could we do? The EPIRB was our only real hope.

R J HAWKE TO THE RESCUE

Hours passed in semi-silence, with the sun beating down on us, and only the noise of the wind and waves. I tried to switch off like a dog with nothing to do, but trying to blank out our situation was nearly impossible. At any second there could be another emergency. We were constantly bouncing around on the end of our sea anchor, not really an ideal time for a spot of meditation! I tried thinking logically, which brought me to only one conclusion: another big wave and we won't be so lucky next time. Then Robin said that if we continue drifting in the same north-westerly direction, we will eventually be due west of the Cocos Islands. Other cruising yachts leaving Cocos heading West to Sri Lanka or the Maldives could possibly intercept our drift line. A long shot, I thought.

What I was more immediately concerned about was the battery life of the EPIRB. In theory we had only 40 hours. The signal had already been active for around 28, which meant the EPIRB would stop in twelve hours, and we only had a few more hours of daylight. Should we turn it off before nightfall and then back on again in the morning? No one would come for us at night, and if the power were left on, the battery would be dead in the morning anyway. When I brought my concerns up with Robin, he immediately agreed that we should turn off the EPIRB once night fell. Then Jeff turned to me again and said,

"What don't you two get? It's all over; no one's coming." Neither Robin nor I said a word for long minutes of silence.

Robin had another idea to steady our dinghy. "JJ, what if we rig up your broken oar and try to make it into a short mast? Then we can use the red plastic rescue sheet as a little sail. It might keep us on the wind a bit, and maybe stop us from getting jerked around so much by the sea anchor. Also, it would be easier to see us with a red plastic sail. What do you reckon?" I thought Robin was just trying to keep our spirits up, but what did we have to lose? So, we kept ourselves busy for another hour. The broken oar was a bit over 1.5 meters long. Together, we rigged up the shortest sailing mast I have ever seen. The base of the oar was lashed in and around the middle of the bench seat. It was a good thing we kept the cord that had held the fender rope. It could now be used to support the mast, and the little holes that had been plugged up with bits of Robin's rubber thongs were an ideal anchor point for the mast side stays.

Next, we had to figure out how to attach the roll-out plastic rescue sheet to the mast and create a functional sail. It was around 4 pm, and the sun was getting lower in the sky. While we were rigging the mast, I was also resigning myself to another night sitting in our dinghy when suddenly, the air above us filled with the most fantastic sound…the scream of a low-flying jet aircraft engine! The coastguard plane flew just a few thousand feet above us. Ripping across the sky, rocking his wings. They have seen us! The EPIRB had worked! A huge lump came up in my throat, hot tears burning in my eyes. "We are not going to die out here!"

The plane reappeared a few minutes later and flew over us, then disappeared over the horizon to the north. Silence again. Robin said, "They didn't drop us an inflatable life raft, so there must be a rescue boat out there somewhere."

We had a full set of rocket parachute flares, so we pulled one out and fired it off up into the wind. These flares were designed to reach up to 300 meters and could be seen around 20 kilometres away. We waited, our eyes all scanning the horizon. Minutes passed, and then we spotted her, a boat maybe 2 or 3 miles away. We waited a while longer, but they were not getting any closer, and then it soon became obvious that they hadn't seen us. We were in a 3-to-4-meter swell with white-capped waves, so I guess we just kept disappearing, mostly out of sight. We decided to launch a second rocket flare, and immediately after it went up, we could see the boat alter course and head directly towards us. Watching our rescue boat grow bigger by the minute was an unbelievable feeling. Then, when she was only a few hundred meters away, they altered course again and closed right in front of us. We tried to wave them off and pointed at our sea anchor, but they misinterpreted our signals and ran right over our floating sea anchor line. Then we heard the clunking sound as our rope wound around and around their props. We were suddenly being dragged towards the boat, and then their engines came to a grinding halt. And then it was all quiet again. We could hear the crew shouting something, but none of us could make out what they were trying to tell us. Our initial jubilation took a sudden, serious turn. Now, we were connected via an umbilical cord, our sea anchor. The crew managed to grab the other end of the anchor rope still attached to the bow of our dinghy and hauled us in, up and over their open stern. Saved! But the remainder of the anchor rope now ran under the stern and was well and truly wrapped around their twin props. Everything had come to a stop.

We were now aboard the R. J. Hawke, the new Cocos Inter-Island ferry and rescue boat. It had only just been commissioned a month before we arrived on Cocos, and named after our prime minister of the day, Bob Hawke.

By this time, it was around 5 pm, and the light was quickly fading. The doctor on board, Edward Bouverie, immediately checked us over, and I think he gave us a drink, some fruit juice. Everyone was elated. I remember I couldn't stand up properly when someone first helped me get out of our dinghy. I was so stiff my legs felt like they wouldn't support me. Then, one of the crew members pulled my life jacket off, wrapped a blanket around me, and helped me into a chair. Bliss! It was unbelievable, but we had been rescued. It had just become a reality. We were saved, but our rescue vessel, the R.J. Hawke, was in serious trouble. She was helpless, drifting, and unable to start. The crew needed to cut off our 10mm sea anchor rope, which was wrapped around their twin props.

MY DIVE MASK TO THE RESCUE

The RJ Hawkes crew were frantically searching through their lockers for a dive mask when they discovered that they didn't have one on board. Initially, I wasn't aware of their problem. When I asked one of the crew what they were looking for, and he said they didn't have a dive mask on board, I immediately sat up and told Edward, the doctor, that I had a dive mask in my grab bag, which was still in the dinghy! Robin also gave the doctor his sharp Opinel sailor's knife, as the crew didn't have a suitable knife on board with a long blade for that sort of job. But now somebody had to get into the water. And it was the doctor, Edward Bouverie, who volunteered to dive over the stern and cut the rope off the props. We all watched on as he had to free dive repeatedly for over 20 minutes in a very risky situation, with just my mask and no snorkel or fins in the fast-fading light.

OUR DINGHY ON THE STERN OF THE R. J. HAWKE

The R.J. Hawke was crippled, drifting and jumping around, the stern slapping the sea, helpless in the three-metre swell. By the time the doctor had managed to cut all the rope off the props, the light was all but gone. He was a very courageous and fit guy, and everyone thanked him for his effort. Then I asked one of the crew if he could get my camera out of the grab bag and take some pics of our Stacer dinghy, now lashed down on the rear deck of the R.J. Hawke. Minutes later, the R.J. Hawke was clear to go. The skipper fired up the engines, and we were back in business. Now there was a 5-6 hour run back to the Cocos Islands. The doctor came back over when he had dried himself off and then checked us all again. One of the crew members pointed out where we could go to the toilet. That made me think it was strange none of us had even been for a pee that I was aware of since we had abandoned Snizort the day before. Taking a roll of toilet paper with us was not really on top of the priority list.

The R.J. Hawke was virtually brand new. Some of the instruments were still wrapped in plastic, and this was her first rescue mission. They were actually in the process of completing sea trials just the day before our rescue. We couldn't have had a better-equipped boat to rescue us. (Apart from forgetting a dive mask!)

One would think this was a great outcome and a good ending to the story, but fate was still playing games. On the way back to Cocos after regaining my sea legs, I asked one of the crew on the bridge what our position was when they found us. He said, "Oh yes, we were just talking about that. Check this out on the chart plotter. It's quite strange. You guys will always be able to locate where Snizort sank in the future because it looks like you sank right on top of the Muirfield subsea mount." The position of this subsea mountain reef is marked on all navigation charts. The peak rises from a depth of 4 kilometres to within only 16 metres of the surface at a latitude of about 13 degrees south of the equator…80 nautical miles southwest of Cocos Islands. It was discovered and named after a cargo ship called the Murfield which hit the mountaintop in a storm and badly damaged the keel. John Jack Paterson, my uncle on board the SS Cerinthus, was torpedoed at about 13 degrees latitude north of the equator. Yet another uncanny coincidence!

BENNY HILL

We finally made it back to Cocos in the early hours of the morning on the 28th. A crowd at the West Island jetty was waiting to greet us. Congratulations were made all around. We were all checked out again and then directed to a government-owned house on the side of the island runway, a place we could use for our accommodation. After completing the initial formalities, I wanted some time to myself, so I left the rest of the crew, telling Robin I needed a walk. I wandered over to the customs building. A cyclone shelter hall at the back doubles as the local cinema. As I approached, I could hear what sounded like a movie, so I walked in and sat down. The projector was running an ABC documentary. The English comedian Benny Hill had recently died. I sat alone for a while in the early hours, trying to absorb everything that had just happened, with the best of Benny Hill showing on the screen. Feeling exhausted but elated at the same time. Eventually, I made my way back to our accommodation and crashed into a blissful sleep.

When I woke up the following day, I experienced a huge adrenaline rush, but I could hardly move, aching all over. At the same time, I felt like I was jumping out of my skin with no more negative thoughts. It was a weird sensation. Yesterday, we were just trying to stay alive, planning the next few hours. Imagine my feeling at waking up safely in a warm bed the following morning. I picked up my diary and wrote across the page. THE PLAN IS LIFE!

There was a small group of tourists on Cocos at the time, and after hearing about our rescue, they raised over 100 dollars and donated some clothing for each of us. There still lots of good people in the world! The doctor, Edward Bouverie, bought our dinghy from Jeff. What happened next was incredible. John Clunnies-Ross once again invited us all to stay at his mansion, Oceania House, on Home Island, and to celebrate our rescue, he organised a banquet for everyone involved.

HOME ISLAND. THE DAY AFTER OUR RESCUE

The meal was a grand affair with over twenty people, including the pilot of the plane and his crew that spotted us, plus the island administration staff seated around a huge oak table in the main hall. Speeches were made, and there was a great feeling of warmth and companionship between us all. The former Malay people from the village served us in their traditional attire. What a fantastic way to end our rescue with a truly memorable night. During the meal, I was seated next to the skipper of the R.J. Hawke. He told me that our EPIRB signal was only just discernible. We were close to 2000 miles off the coast of Western Australia, the very edge of the EPIRB's range, when our distress signal was first picked up by a satellite and then relayed to the Australian Maritime Safety Authority in Canberra. They initially thought our signal was just an echo because it was so weak and in such a remote location (probably because of the broken antenna). They waited until after several satellite passes to confirm the signal to be sure before activating the rescue mission. We were so very, very lucky.

Jeff, of course, was not as happy or in the same frame of mind as Robin and me. We had lost all of our personal belongings on board, including my gemstones from Singapore and other items. Everything went down with Snizort. However, Jeff had lost his boat, and we later heard that Snizort was not insured. Naturally, at the time, there was considerable empathy for Jeff. (I did hear on the grapevine that he had also borrowed thousands of dollars for the project to get Snizort back to Australia, a total financial disaster.) He really started to lose it, hitting the bottle hard. Then, a couple of days later, while Robin and I were playing cards in our accommodation, Jeff marched in after what looked like a long session at the bar. When he first opened our cabin door, we both looked up at him, swaying unsteadily in the doorway. He stared at Robin for a moment and said, "You know there's absolutely no chance you two will get paid!". I just looked on, shrugged my shoulders, but said nothing. Robin slowly nodded. Under the circumstances, neither Robin nor I were surprised. Neither of us expected to be paid. Maybe Jeff thought there would be a different reaction from us…I don't know. Jeff turned and walked out, slamming the door behind him.

I thought, no matter how depressed or bad he felt about losing his boat, this was the most ungracious person I had ever met in my life. Jeff seemed to forget the fact that the boat he built split open and nearly killed us all, and if it hadn't been for Robin taking charge in a near-life-or-death situation, we would not have survived. I had expected that at some point, he would have at least acknowledged it was Robin and his excellent sea knowledge that saved our lives. Still, I never heard Jeff once thank Robin or recognise his contribution to our survival. There was no mention of Robin in his official report to the Australian Maritime Authorities regarding the loss of Snizort. Even so, we both still felt for Jeff as he had lost so much. But our relationship was over. Finished. Neither Robin nor I bothered speaking to Jeff again after the incident regarding the pay. Personally, I didn't care about the money. I was flat broke, but at the same time, I felt like a million dollars, with a new sense of freedom and a release, no longer obligated as a crew member. I was back in charge of my fate, and I felt great!

Then, another problem arose. We were called to a meeting on West Island with the island administrator, Barry Cunningham. I suppose it was because we were a professional delivery crew that the Cocos Island administration informed us the federal government in Canberra was considering charging us for all the costs related to the rescue, which amounted to many thousands of dollars. Incredible! On top of losing everything, another blow. Jeff was shaking and looked stunned- just what he didn't need to hear. We all stopped and took a breath. I thought for a moment, then pointed out that there had recently been another rescue of an Indonesian fishing boat crew after their boat sank near Cocos only a month before our rescue. We had heard about that incident when we first arrived. The fishermen were repatriated to Indonesia at no charge and even given some cash each. So why should a tax-paying Australian crew have to pay for the same privilege? The commissioner soon realised this situation could get messy, and that you can't get blood out of a stone. Jeff hardly said a word. He looked pale and unsteady, like he was on edge and ready to crash- a mental breakdown? It was easy to see he needed help, or at least some professional care.

The successful rescue had been broadcast across media all over Australia, so I guess they didn't want to end the saga on a sour note. We had absolutely nothing left anyway. After contacting Canberra, the administrator,

Barry Cunningham, informed us that we would all be repatriated to the Australian mainland on the next available flight at no charge. What a relief! I asked my friend, Dieter, the customs officer responsible for arranging our flight back to Australia, to seat Robin and me as far apart as possible from Jeff. He understood the issue between us.

The Cocos Island administration on West Island consisted of a relatively small group of about 30 expats and their families. As I mentioned before, there was only one bar on West Island, in the customs building, the social hub. I heard Jeff's drinking binges had earned him the reputation as 'The angry Aussie.'

When we finally boarded our flight back to Perth later in the week, Robin and I sat at the opposite end of the plane to Jeff. Shortly after returning to Perth, we parted ways and never heard from Jeff again.

13 MONTHS LATER

Despite our near-fatal ordeal, Robin and I decided to continue with our marine delivery business. I figured we had been pre-disastered, so the chances of another sinker were slim. When we first returned to Fremantle, the story of our rescue made the front pages of the local newspaper, so I kept a few copies. A couple of pages in another short story caught my attention. The article stated that a local fisherman had likely fallen off his boat in Cockburn Sound, just a few kilometres off the coast of Fremantle. The fisherman's boat was found drifting miles up the coast, and his body washed ashore a couple of days later. That made me reflect again on all the drama we had been through and still survived against what seemed like impossible odds. The poor guy probably just lost his balance in sight of home.

CHRISTINA

Life returned to some sort of normal. Feeling so positive, I joined a dinner date club called 'Dinner for Six'. Call it fate or being in the right place at the right time, I believe something serendipitous happened. The meal had been organised at a local French restaurant. As usual I was running a little late, and ended up with the only empty seat at the table. Next to me was seated a sweet lady by the name of Christina. A very attractive redhead, she reminded me of someone, but I couldn't put my finger on it. But that wasn't the key. When we started talking it felt like I was catching up with a long-lost friend. Then she told me she was interested in sailing and had just started a sailing course on the Swan River.

A little later that evening, we were discussing our childhood years and realised we had grown up only a few miles apart on the other side of the world, in the north of England. As a child, Christina and her parents would holiday in their caravan at Filey Bay, just a couple of miles up the coast from my hometown of Bridlington, a seaside holiday resort located in Heartbeat Country on the East

Yorkshire coast. As I listened to Christina's bubbling conversation, it came to me. 'Gilligan's Island'—Christina had a strong resemblance to one of the show's stars, the sexy movie star character, Ginger. By the end of our first meal, I had asked Christina if she would like to come for a Saturday afternoon race around the cans, out in the sound off the Fremantle Sailing Club. "Yes, I'd love to. That sounds like fun."

What followed was nearly our first and last date. I arranged with a friend, Matt, who owned a fifty-foot sloop, for us to join his crew the approaching weekend. Christina was as keen as mustard. I assured her it would be a champagne cruise as Matt's yacht, Salacious, had a huge open cockpit with a circular lounge. "You'll have a ball, and we can have drinks after the race at the club."

My carefully planned strategy to entice Christina was going according to plan until we arrived at the club. Christina looked hot and came dressed, looking the part in her black and white striped top, white capri jeans, and copper locks tucked under a cute baseball cap. As we walked into the bar together, Matt caught us. "Sorry guys, Salacious has an engine problem, but if you still want to go sailing, George is short of crew on Battlestar." I had heard about Battlestar but never had a chance to sail with them. George, the owner, had imported Battlestar, a 45ft aluminium Admiral's Cup racing yacht from the UK. I told Christina, "If you still want to go, I think we're in for a ride. I heard Battlestar goes like a rocket." So, we walked out along the jetty to Battlestar's pen.

George, whom I had previously met at the bar, welcomed us aboard. As we climbed on deck, it was apparent this was not going to be the champagne cruise I had promised. This was a professional racing setup with twin coffee grinder winches, a flat deck layout, and running backstays. George was a nice guy but a serious racing skipper. His crew all had their jobs but guests were just ballast to George, and had to hang over the side. Christina was okay initially, sitting on the rail as we cleared out of the club. Then, the afternoon sea breeze picked up, and we were off. George asked me if I could look after one of the coffee grinders and help with the running backstays when we went about. Christina was hanging on the side as Battlestar heeled over and accelerated out into Cockburn Sound. I became totally absorbed in my job and didn't have much time for Christina, who had to scuttle back and forth across the deck to the other rail each time we tacked. At one stage, we hit 12 knots, ploughing through the sea, white water rushing over the open alloy deck. Battlestar easily won the race, and everyone was high-fiving as we crossed the finishing line.

Then I turned to look for Christina, and oops, I knew I was in trouble. The hat was gone, her hair was all stuck around her face, she was soaking wet, and her white jeans were covered in dirty marks. I got an icy cold stare. She was really angry and on the verge of tears. On the way back to the club, there wasn't anything I could say to make things right. I had neglected her. Apologies were too late, and hardly a word was said as she jumped in her car and drove off. We both laugh about that day now, but it really was touch and go whether she would finally return my pleading calls and give me another chance.

When we first met, who would have thought that Christina would eventually join Robin and me on several deliveries? The three of us would sail thousands of miles together after that first meal. Christina also became a very competent sailor, and as she was a qualified chef, Robin and I shared some great meals onboard. The confines of a small cruising yacht for weeks of open ocean sailing must be one of the ultimate tests for any couple's relationship.

Christina invited me to her place for a meal one evening. Months had slipped by, and our relationship had grown stronger. We were enjoying a glass of wine and having an in-depth conversation when there was yet another one of those 'OMG' moments. Christina gave me a serious look and said, "JJ, there's something I have been wanting to tell you for a while now. I have been trying to find the right moment, and it's really weird: my previous husband, David, died on the same weekend that you were rescued off the Cocos Islands." That floored me. I was speechless. There was nothing anyone could say when you hear something like that.

SCALLYWAG

So, time slipped by, and I thought I had moved on from the Snizort saga—just an intriguing part of my sailing past. How wrong can we sometimes be? Little did I know another chapter was about to unfold, again awaiting me on the Cocos Keeling Islands. Another international job came up: For business reasons, Ashley, the owner, had left his yacht in a foreign marina twelve months earlier. Scallywag, his 36ft sloop, was moored on the Malaysian Coast at the the Royal Selangor Yacht Club, Port Klang, again positioned in the Straits of Malacca, roughly 3 degrees north of the equator.

After the Snizort job, I decided that recording all the long-distance deliveries was a good idea, so a diary has always accompanied me. This delivery would be just Robin and me, double-handed. Once all the paperwork was out of the way, Ashley arranged to fly us up to Kuala Lumpur on the 18th of August. Christina had also arranged to fly back to the UK, leaving on the same day. So, after hugs and promises, we flew our separate ways. At that time, we had been together for about eight months, so this break would be the first big test of our relationship. Ashley would fly up and join us when we got to Kuala Lumpur. Then, we would travel to the Port Klang marina together to familiarise ourselves with Scallywag, a UK-built 36 ft fibreglass, centre cockpit, Moody designed cruising yacht. Once we had resolved any problems with the boat, Ashley would leave us there and return to his work in Australia.

CUSTOMS DETAIN ROBIN

On landing after a nine-hour flight from Perth to Kuala Lumpur, we immediately ran into problems with customs. I hold dual British and Australian passports, so as Malaysia was once part of the British Commonwealth, I had no issues entering the country and walked through customs without a hitch. Not so easy for Robin, who only had his Australian passport. The customs officer wanted to know why he only had a one-way ticket into the country and no entry visa. We didn't think that was necessary since we only planned to be in Malaysia for a few days. We got that wrong! Ashley should have pre-arranged a cruising visa for us. Not a good start, but nothing ever seems to go to plan initially

There was another problem. Robin had no physical proof or paperwork to demonstrate that he was contracted as a delivery skipper. Consequently, he was taken away and spent a few hours in the customs detention centre while I contacted Ashley. Hours later, at 3am, Ashley finally managed to get in touch with the KL customs officers. Robin was free to go. After a very, very long day with numerous hassles, it was wonderful to collapse into a hotel bed. Ashley flew in overnight and picked us up mid-morning.

ROYAL SELANGOR YACHT CLUB

After a late breakfast, our taxi took us 30 kilometres west from Kuala Lumpur to the coast and the Royal Selangor Yacht Club. As we drove down into the marina, the first sight to greet us was the king of Malaysia's mini ocean liner, moored alongside the main wharf. Also tied up at the jetty, nestled under the regal bows of His Highness's yacht, was Scallywag, which looked good- a pleasant surprise! My first impressions were very positive. Ashley had sailed her all the way from the UK with his partner and friends, so we planned to take her out for sea trials later in the day after charging the batteries.

Scallywag's engine was a Volvo turbocharged diesel, which was a bit noisy, but generally, the boat seemed to be in surprisingly good condition. Quite luxurious, I thought. And we had a functioning autopilot for a change. Ashley had also pre-arranged a full service for the boat. He was very professional and paid us 1,000 US in advance for the delivery, with the balance to be paid upon completion of the job.

With all the formalities out of the way, a drink at the Royal Selangor Yacht Club was calling. The bar was a stunning mix of exotic teak and wooden inlays, with some fantastic sculptures. Fit for a king! The bar manager said, "His Highness is a frequent visitor to the club". we sat down with Ashley and established a regular UHF radio communication schedule. So far, this job has been progressing in textbook fashion. Ashley was one of those amiable individuals who possessed excellent communication skills. It is the kind of relationship you would hope for between the owner and the delivery crew. There must be mutual trust and respect. After all, you're sailing away with his extremely expensive toy, and God knows where you could take it.

Breakdowns were another point to consider. If the boat engine fails or you lose electrical, power living on board in the tropics becomes impossible without a water pump, refrigeration, or lighting. So, there must be a clear understanding regarding accommodation costs if a breakdown occurs. All these scenarios were ironed out with Ashley over a few beers at the marina bar. It was getting late. Ashley left for his hotel, and then we had a short walk along the jetty. And I was looking forward to our first night on board. As we approached Scallywag, the bows of the royal yacht towered over us. I said to Robin, "This delivery is by royal decree." When we climbed on board and checked out the accommodation, a smile came to my face. I had a comfortable bed in my own cabin, and I even had a fan.

Robin was happy with the navigation equipment, which included a new, up-to-date chart plotter. Ashley came down the next morning and double-checked to make sure all our paperwork was in order. He wished us good luck and then left us at the marina. We fuelled up, and I went shopping for a week's provisions. After couple of drinks at the marina bar that night with the locals, we were nearly set. Robin, as usual, was busy with the navigation charts. The next morning, I had a quick look below the water line. There was a bit of algae growth, but it was easy to clean up with a scouring pad. Half an hour in the water, and Scallywag had a slippery bum. We were good to go, and I was really looking forward to this delivery.

DAY ONE AGAIN

After all the problems we had with Snizort getting through the busy shipping lanes, Robin figured we would have an easier run west over the top of Sumatra if we kept to the Malaysian coast for a further 150kms's north past Langkawi. We decided to make our departure point for Cocos from the Ao Chalong marina on the Southern tip of Phuket, Thailand, located about 8 degrees north of the Equator.

We motored out of Port Klang around 3pm with no wind, as usual. Another two hours motoring through the channel, and we were past all the local islands and back out into the Straits of Malacca, heading north as the day faded into another tropical night. Scallywag's turbo diesel was apparently very economical, but unlike most yacht engines, high revving, and a bit of a screamer. I decided to look at the Volvo engine manual and discovered it would need an oil change every fifty hours of running time. Not a problem if you are just motoring out of a marina for a few minutes and then hoisting the sails. Fifty hours of engine time could take a year to accumulate, but we were looking at 2,000 km, mainly in the doldrums, with a possible oil change every two or three days. Pumping oil out of a hot diesel engine is a difficult job on a yacht at sea and not a good place to be, especially for those who get seasick. Thankfully, our first oil change would be at anchor after we arrived at Phuket, 500 kilometres north of our present position. So, all bases were now covered. A beautiful yacht to deliver and money in the bank. I thought about Christina. Oh yes, she would have loved to be a part of this new adventure.

Those first few hours into the night felt good. The ocean was flat-calm with spectacular sheet lightning silhouetting the fishing boats, Scallywag's wake, a glowing phosphorescent line in the sea trailed for a hundred meters astern. I experienced the inner feeling that I was living life to the max. We rounded the NW coast of

Penang Island, 75 miles north of Port Klang, at dawn. When I checked the bilges at the change of watch, they were dry, but there was a faint smell of burning rubber coming from the engine room!

PROBLEMS, PROBLEMS.

Robin came on watch while I went down below and pulled off the engine cover. The alternator belt was frayed, loose and slipping badly. Either it hadn't been properly adjusted and tensioned by whoever did the service in Port Klang, or we should have checked after a few hours of motoring for any stretching. It's hard to think of everything. Whatever, we had no choice but to turn off the engine so we could change the belts. I knew we had a couple of spares, but stopping in these conditions with very little wind would leave us drifting, unable to manoeuvre or get out of the way of any approaching vessels. Robin stayed at the helm while I located the belts, and then we shut down the Volvo. Scallywag immediately slowed and started a gentle rolling motion, our main sail flogging in the hot tropical air. The belt change only took me around 20 minutes, but the smell of burnt rubber and hot diesel oil was enough to turn the hardiest sailor's stomach. By the time I made it back on deck, I was bathed in sweat and retching. Robin just grinned and restarted Scallywag. The joys of sailing!

I was about to grab a drink, cool down and relax when Robin told me we now had another problem. The voltage meter was not showing a charge. This time I stayed at the helm while Robin went below, checking to see if I had missed anything. He returned on deck a few minutes later and said, "Everything looks OK to me, JJ. It's only another 180k's north to Langkawi. Let's just get there and then worry about the voltage regulator." "Sounds good to me," I said. I spent the rest of the day with a few cold beers soaking up the life of the Straits. To save batteries, our autopilot was switched off as we needed the power for navigation lights and GPS. Autopilots are great, but they chew up lots of juice. So were back to manual helming.

After motoring all night, on of 23rd August, we made our way into Bass Harbour and back into the Langkawi marina moorings. It was around 8am and another tropical downpour greeted us. I went forward and let the anchor go. Robin was running Scallywag in reverse to set the anchor when I heard the end of the anchor chain rattling up the hawser pipe and onto the deck. I tried to grab the chain and yelled out to Robin, "Stop, go forward". The wet chain was running through my hands in the downpour with no chance of holding it. The end of the chain should have been attached to the bulkhead in the anchor locker, which would have prevented this from happening. Instead, there was a big loop of nylon rope about a meter long tied onto the last link. I just managed to flick the rope loop over the capstan head. It stretched taught but held. Robin waved from the cockpit and gave me a thumbs-up as we came to a wet stop. We would have lost our only anchor and all the chain. I now understand the meaning of the term 'the bitter end'. It worked out as we only had 20 meters of chain anyway. Ashley forgot to warn us about the unusually short length of the unattached anchor chain.

Our batteries were showing very low, so Robin wanted to keep the Volvo running in case we couldn't restart it. The alternator was also smoking hot after running for so many hours. There was no choice but to shut down the engine. All was quiet. The difference without the constant turbo engine noise was amazing. With Scallywag safely at anchor, we could both relax as we had made it this far.

Robin called customs to clear us in. While we were waiting for them to arrive, we inflated the rubber dinghy and attached our five-hp outboard. Once customs were cleared, we made our way ashore and attempted to locate an electrician, but when we made initial inquiries, it turned out that we had arrived at the start of a 3-day Muslim religious period. No one was allowed to work, and everything in town was closed, and I mean everything. Scallywag wasn't going anywhere until we get our power problems sorted out. On top of all this, Robin told me he had a bad toothache and thought he might have an abscess. The dream job had only just begun but turned into crap within a couple of days!

I thought about my agent friend Zach from our previous visit to Langkawi. I still had his card so I gave him a ring. He was very happy to hear from me but told me he couldn't do any work till the weekend after the religious holiday period. He did put me onto another Australian guy, Paul, at the marina, which was the only place where anything was happening. Zac also proudly announced "JJ, Allah has blessed me with my fourth wife" Incredible!

Back at the marina, Robin was sitting at the bar, killing the pain from his tooth with rum. I didn't blame him, really, but it wasn't a lot of help. First, I called Ashley to bring him up to date and tell him we needed money to cover the new expenses. Our original plan was just to fuel up and leave. Now, if we stayed, we paid. There was also another problem. I discovered after making inquiries at the marina that to transfer money into my Visa account, I would first need to open a Malaysian bank account. Everything was getting too hard. So, I called Ashley back and told him I would use my credit card to get whatever we needed. Ashley agreed that he would get the money sorted out with me and arrange for a new alternator when arrived at the Ao Chalong marina in Phuket.

My next job was to call Aussie Paul at the marina. about finding a genset so we could charge our batteries. He sounded like an over-the-top, friendly type of guy. We decided to meet at the bar first thing the next day. There was nothing else we could do for the rest of the day so we wandered around town and enjoyed the sights of Langkawi.

The following morning, I caught up with Paul at the marina bar. A lean, bronze 50-something with scruffy blonde hair, he didn't stop talking from the moment I said hello. Paul told me he had a generator and it was on his boat, so after a coffee, we went down along the jetty and out to his 45ft yacht. He was living alone on board a nice boat, but it looked a bit neglected, in a generally run-down condition. When we went below deck, there were several small outboards and generators in various states of repair, all up in the forward cabin area. I didn't get a good feeling. Paul could see my apprehension and reassured me it was all his stuff. He was a marine mechanic who got stuck in Langkawi and just ran out of money. As they say, at the end of the day, 'beggars can't be choosers.' We settled on a price. I think I bought a slightly warm Honda generator. Paul agreed to service the generator and deliver it to Scallywag the following morning.

It was stinking hot and nothing was working on Scallywag without power, so we spent another night on shore in the luxury of a couple of air-conditioned rooms. That night I got smashed at the marina bar with Robin. The next morning, we were both really hungover. At least Robin had managed to acquire a packet of strong painkillers, some antibiotics, and a good supply of rum.

After breakfast, we went aboard Scallywag with the rubber duck. Robin was not well at all. His face was swollen up on one side. Our supplies and extra fuel for the generator needed to be loaded by 10am. Paul showed up with the Honda generator, which had to be securely lashed down forward of the mast, leaving little room on deck. Everything became a major struggle in the heat, but at least we were on board with our dead-flat batteries. Once the genset was kicked into gear and running smoothly, Paul waved us goodbye and said we could call him back if there were any problems. Next, we needed to connect the gen-set to our main battery bank with long jumper leads. I had already disconnected the alternator belt, but we needed power for refrigeration and navigation lights, so the Honda was kept running on charge. Even our gas stove didn't work without power, as it was connected through the gas detector safety system in the bilges.

Naturally, Robin wanted to charge our batteries before we left to make sure our hot Honda genset got a good test run. After four hours of continuous charging, there was enough juice in the batteries to start the Volvo, but when we tried the starter, nothing happened. Perhaps it was because the alternator was disconnected. Unfortunately, I have never been great with electrics. After checking all the other connections without success, jump-starting the Volvo was our only option. The throb of a yacht engine humming along at sea is generally not unpleasant, but the noise from the Volvo wasn't music to anyone's ears. (I decided if I ever bought a yacht, it would never have a turbo diesel).

MONKEY ISLAND

We were anchored in Bass Harbour next to the marina jetty. From here, we again must make the passage west through the channel of picturesque islands that opened into the Straits of Malacca. It was 3 pm. I raised the anchor by hand. The winch would have eaten up too much juice. After numbing his tooth, Robin was back to his navigation. He planned to shelter Scallywag in a bay behind a tiny island at the end of the channel overnight, then head north in the morning back into the Malacca Straits channel.

As we were leaving Bass Harbour, we had a fair wind for a change and a beautiful day to sail through the islands. An hour and a half later, we dropped the sails and motored around the back of a little island into a tiny U-shaped Bay with a white sandy beach surrounded by dense green jungle, monkeys running up and down the palm trees, screaming at the new intruders. We dropped the anchor in clear shallow water on a sandy bottom 20 meters from the beach just before dark, and to save power, we tied a fluorescent reading light to the mast for an anchor light. A peaceful the end to a very long day. Honda off, Volvo off, just the monkeys watching us. We are quiet, they are quiet.

Most ocean-going cruising yachts seem to accumulate a bit of a library over time, and Scallywag had a couple of sailing books by my favourite maritime author of the day, Tristan Jones, an ex-delivery skipper and author of some of the almost unbelievable voyages I have ever read. I picked up one of his first published books. 'The Incredible Voyage.' Reading with a headlight, I just made the first couple of pages, then fell into a weary sleep as Scallywag gently rocked in our sheltered anchorage. Our idyllic little bay was the perfect backdrop for breakfast on deck the following day.

From our tiny island position to Ao Chalong, Phuket was roughly 100 nautical miles north. The starter motor electrics were still not working. So, again, we had to jumpstart the Volvo. Immediately after we fired up our engine the monkeys woke up and started screaming goodbye to us. The breeze picked up as we motored around the island and back into the straights. We had another fantastic day sailing north through those crazy limestone column islands, some only meters wide and towering thirty meters out of the sea, dripping over the top with green jungle cover. Sea eagles were swooping down around us, hitting the water and grabbing fish just below the surface with their razor-sharp talons. I wasn't having any luck with my fishing gear, so between watches, I immersed myself back into the Tristan Jones book I had started the previous night.

What a sailing legend! Over 400,000 logged nautical miles. No other sailor before him or since has ever come close. I heard that he kept right on sailing after losing a leg when he was hit by a tram in Holland. He called his next yacht, a catamaran, The Outward Leg. That tickled me. I thought he must have had a really bent sense of humour. We had a favourable wind all that day, but Robin didn't want to risk turning off the engine again. So, we motor-sailed all day and on into the night. I stayed on watch for 8 hours to let Robin get some sleep and relief from his toothache. It was intense and absorbing, picking my way through the towering islands to the next waypoint. Everything looked surreal, silhouetted in the moonlight. It was an eerie and unique experience, and I appreciated the time Robin put into the navigation work to set up the waypoints.

As the tropical dawn broke, we arrived at Ao Chalong, Phuket, around 6 a.m. Quite a sight! The bay was just starting to come to life. About four or five miles across and just north of Ko Lon Island. There were hundreds of yachts on moorings, along with some big luxury powerboats, a fleet of fishing boats, the usual ferries, tourist boats, and longtails, creating a busy, colourful early morning scene, with lots of traffic on the water.

Once we cleared customs, I contacted Ashley. His friend, Mark, who was supposed to meet us here, would not be able to make it until after the weekend. Robin couldn't see a dentist until Monday, either. We did manage to locate an electrician in Phuket, and he would visit us at

10am. on Monday. I called Ashley back, and he asked if I could open a bank account in Phuket so he could transfer some money to me. Banks are closed on weekends; so once again we were stuck. After all the drama, Robin gave it up and made a path to the lighthouse marina bar. The bar was the main haunt for all the visiting boat crews and featured a red and white striped mini lighthouse above the entrance, about 10 meters high.

MR JIT

Chilling out with a couple of beers is probably the best option when you just can't win, so I decided to join him. We had only downed our first drink when a Thai guy introduced himself to me as Mr Jit, Personal Agent and Tour Guide. (I must have had a sign across my forehead). As this was my first trip to Thailand and I didn't know my way around, and as I had the rest of the weekend to kill, I thought, why not? The next couple of days I spent exploring Phuket with the help of my new agent friend. He told me his name, translated to English, was Alex. We spent hours wandering through markets, around temples with golden, reclining Buddhas and getting to know Phuket -doing the tourist thing.

TEMPTATION

At mid-morning Mr Jit drove me over to his friend's restaurant on Patong Beach for lunch. When we walked in through the front door, I was looking straight into the eyes of a stunning Thai lady. She gave me a killer smile and then glided over to our table as we sat down. She leaned over the table and said something to Mr Jit. He laughed and then introduced me. I can't remember her name, but I do remember she had a soft, sexy voice. Then

Mr Jit asked me, with a knowing grin, if I thought that she was 'Suay' (Beautiful) and if I would like to have a personal guide and companion while I was in Phuket for 1000 baht a day (about 50 Australian Dollars at the time). OMG, so very tempting, but I thought about Christina. She was on the other side of the world, and my track record wasn't very good with relationships. I had all sorts of lurid thoughts running through my head, but I really didn't want to screw things up again. I was also fully aware that in Phuket, a personal companion became a part-time wife and expected to be wined and dined and entertained in a Western-style. I didn't think she would have been too impressed living on Scallywag and sharing the boat with Robin onboard. So, I put the fantasy thoughts out of my head and politely declined. I was beginning to wonder if my new friend Mr Jit was a part-time pimp! The Thais are just so very polite.

It was late Sunday afternoon when Mr Jit dropped me back at the lighthouse bar where I caught up with Robin. He had been recuperating there with his aching tooth all weekend, partially anaesthetised. So, I decided to settle in for a few ales with him. I pulled up a chair. Robin was sitting at a table and having a drink with some old sailing mates. He was the proverbial skipper who seemed to know someone in every port of call.

TRISTAN JONES

While we were seated, the bar suddenly went quiet. I turned around to see a little old guy being pushed in a wheelchair entering the bar. He had a full grey beard, a skipper's hat and looked around 70. It was evident he had no legs. Robin leaned over to me and said, "Guess who that is?" To my amazement, it was Tristan Jones, and he was being treated like royalty. The lighthouse tavern bar was relatively small. When someone offered to buy him a drink he declined and said in a low, hushed voice, "I'll just have a juice, thanks." One of Robin's friends, who also knew Tristan, said, "He wouldn't be drinking alcohol anyway as he had recently adopted the Muslim faith." He added Tristan had recently changed his name and was now known as Ali something or other. Robin, of course, had also met Tristan years before on one of his many voyages. He glanced over in our direction, recognised his old friends, and made his way to our table to say hello. I was introduced.

Wow! I was sitting at a table having a drink and a casual conversation with Tristan Jones and a bunch of his old sailing mates. He certainly didn't fit the image I had created in my head. Initially he didn't say much. His deep-set, heavy-lidded eyes and craggy face had that exposed to the elements, salt-weathered old sailor's look. It was hard to imagine that this was the sailing superman whose stories I couldn't put down.

He was quite friendly and eventually asked me what I was doing there, so I related our story to him. We were a delivery crew stuck in Phuket with a broken boat on our way back to Australia. Then he asked me how long I thought it would take to get Scallywag fixed before we left Thailand. The reason he asked was because someone had pinched the Thai ensign off his yacht, and he was wondering if when we left Phuket, we would still need ours. Robin piped in. He told Tristan he was more than welcome to our Thai ensign once Scallywag was repaired.

Tristan's boat, a very unusual 40 ft catamaran, was moored in Ao Chalong Bay, not far from where Scallywag was anchored, so we had a loose arrangement to catch up with him later in the week. Then Tristan waved for a Thai carer to come over and push the wheelchair for him. As he left the bar Robin's friend mentioned that Tristan had been quite depressed lately and was not his old self since losing his other leg to an infection the year before. What I initially thought would be a really boring weekend stuck on the boat turned out to be full of surprises.

When we returned to Scallywag later in the afternoon, another 45ft cruising Yacht Isa Lea had moored close alongside us. We couldn't see anyone on board, and it looked like they had already gone ashore. Robin and I were getting a meal together when we noticed that our new neighbour was dragging her anchor and slowly sliding by with the tide. The bottom there was thick, soft mud. We tried to shout across but couldn't raise anyone, so we got back into our rubber duck and went over. The boat was all locked up and as there was no one on board. We found another spare anchor lashed on deck, so we tied a line through the stock and back through the anchor chain. Then we let out more chain manually and threw it all over, creating a double anchor set-up. We waited on board for a few minutes, and she seemed to be holding, so Robin left a note in the cockpit for the owner. Then we went back to Scallywag for dinner. We joked that maybe the crew had run into Mr Jit and his girls or booked into a hotel and hit the nightlife at Patong Beach.

Monday morning came around, and by 10 am we had disconnected the alternator and the drive belts, ready for the electrician, but he didn't show. Ashley then contacted us on the radio phone, saying that his friend Mark would arrive the next day, Tuesday. Robin needed to see a dentist, and I needed to open a bank account in Phuket, so we caught a tuk-tuk (motorised rickshaw) downtown. Fortunately, dentists were very reasonably priced in Phuket, so once Robin was sorted out, I headed across to the local Thai bank, opening an account with the minimum allowed amount of 50 US dollars. I asked the teller when I could expect to receive the transfer of funds from Australia to my new Thai bank account. It was then I discovered bank policy meant I could deposit money into my account, but I would not be able to make a withdrawal for a period of one calendar month. Great! This account was useless to me. I said goodbye to my $50 US dollars.

By this time, I was 1000 dollars into my visa card and it was nearly maxed out. I had given Robin $100 dollars for the dentist, then gifted my last $50 to the bank. At times like these, when everything seems to work out wrong no matter what you do, it's best to just go with the flow. Phuket being so stinking hot only made the situation worse. I gave up. It was time to head back to Scallywag and get on the radio phone. Once I contacted Ashley and explained the situation with the bank, he told me that he would transfer $1500 US to me through his friend Mark. Also, Mark would cover our accommodation expenses and take the alternator to be repaired. Robin's tooth was on the mend. The pressure seemed to be off. It was time to unwind and head back to the lighthouse marina bar.

END OF THE LINE

After our frequent visits, Robin and I were beginning to feel like locals, and there were always a few other expats in the bar. One afternoon I had a conversation with a couple of Aussies living aboard their yachts. When I inquired about the large amount of cruising boats in the bay, one said, "Phuket mate, it's sort of the end of the line. There are a lot of boats out there waiting for a delivery crew."

His friend chipped in. "It's like this. After yachties do their big trip from Australia to Singapore and then cruise up through the Malacca Straights and the islands, there is very limited cruising ground to the north along this coast after Phuket. North of here is the Andaman Sea, which is not exactly friendly waters for yachties. It is Burmese government controlled with extreme political restrictions. If you get your paperwork wrong you can be arrested, thrown in jail, with your boat possibly confiscated. Another destination around 400 miles to the northwest of Phuket are the remote Nicobar Islands. There is nothing much there, with no fuel or any other infrastructure facilities. The indigenous island inhabitants have a reputation for being fiercely territorial and aggressive. I even heard of visiting yachts having spears thrown at them! Once past the Nicobar Islands, you're out into the Bay of Bengal heading towards India or Sri Lanka. So, for the majority of cruising yachts, Phuket is the natural end of the line. To get your yacht home from here, you either go back the way you came from the south, or head west over the top of Sumatra, (as we were preparing to do), then south 1100 nautical miles to the Cocos Keeling Islands. From there it is another 2000 miles of non - stop sailing, mainly against the wind, to Perth, West Australia. The only other alternative to getting a boat home is to have it loaded on a ship as deck cargo…a very expensive exercise. So Phuket is a bit like a craypot, mate. She's easy to get into, but hard to get out of!"

MARK

Ashley's friend Mark turned out to be a really nice guy, another switched-on 40-something Aussie, very reassuring and a great help. After our initial get-together over a coffee, it was great for us to hear that we didn't have to worry about living expenses or getting Scallywag fixed. He was a local businessman and obviously knew his way around. After coffee, we handed Mark the alternator, and he took off into town, telling us he would get the alternator checked out and catch up with us later in the day. So, we wandered around town and familiarised ourselves with a couple of local bars and the CBD of Phuket. Four hours passed. Mark turned up with some unexpected news. The alternator was badly salt-damaged, irreparable, and of course, a replacement was not available locally in Phuket. He told us a new alternator would have to be ordered, and it would probably take two or three days, maybe a week, to come by train from Bangkok. I thought this was turning out to be a very expensive stop for Ashley, but there was nothing we could do to speed things up and get Scallywag on her way home. Until then, Robin and I hadn't worried too much about our day-to-day costs, and as everybody ate out, I decided to keep a log of all our receipts and expenses. Despite all the delays, the day ended well when Mark reappeared with a big smile on his face. "This should keep you guys happy," and handed me $1500 US dollars cash.

In the days that followed, while we were waiting for the alternator to arrive, the electrician finally showed up and went right through Scallywag's electrical system. We hoped that once the new alternator was installed our power problems will be over. Lucky for us Mark was the perfect agent to have in Phuket, and also, being Ashley's friend meant we didn't have to try to justify or explain to Ashley the reason for all the expensive delays.

ONE MAN CHANGES A CULTURE!

I ran into my friend Mr Jit again at the lighthouse bar and we slipped into a discussion about Tristan Jones after I mentioned that we were going to leave our Thai flag with Tristan when we left Phuket. When I first mentioned Tristan Jones, he really lit up and said that Tristan was a very famous and popular man in Phuket, and how he alone had changed the Thai culture. Then Mr Jit told me this incredible story:

In 1987, not long after Tristan first arrived in Phuket, he organised a group of disabled people into a crew and then took them all by boat on a fantastic adventure. At that time, he still had one leg. The voyage started along the Andaman seacoast just North of Phuket, into a river mouth, and followed it upstream into the highlands. With the help of locals and elephants, they dragged their small boat over a narrow neck of land called the Kra Isthmus, about 500 meters high. Once over the mountain ridge, they dragged their boat down to where they could reconnect with another major river system. Tristan and his disabled crew then slowly made their way downstream right through to the Gulf of Thailand on the east coast, where they were met by a crowd of locals and journalists, who then brought them triumphantly to Bangkok to be celebrated by the media. According to Mr Jit, that was the first time ever that disabled or crippled people had been publicly recognised in Thai culture.

When Mr Jit finished his conversation, I asked the obvious question: why? Mr Jit explained that the majority of Thai people followed Buddhism, and at the time, according to Buddha's teaching, if you were crippled or deformed, this was punishment for having been a bad person in a previous life. Mr Jit told me deformed or crippled people were kept out of sight, and some were chained up like dogs at the back of the house because of a cleft pallet or some other natural deformity. But Tristan was not finished there, he noticed that none of the major hotels in Bangkok at that time had any facilities for people with disabilities. So, he convinced them they were missing out on millions of tourist dollars by not providing for this clientele. In today's world, all these facilities are taken for granted.

Tristan also helped to found the Atlantic Society for disabled people in Thailand. All the royalties from his books go to the disabled. As our conversation with Mr Jit came to an end, I asked him how come he knew so much about Tristan Jones. Mr Jit bent down and pulled up his trouser leg to expose a huge, ragged, shiny white scar around his lower right leg, just above his ankle. He said, "JJ, when I was a boy, I nearly lost my foot after an accident with a machete." He told me his mother would hide him at home, out of sight, away from friends and family for months, till he could walk again. Tristan had set all those people free.

Tristan's final book was the story of this journey with his disabled crew, titled 'To Venture Further'. Tristan's voyages and his books had some very vocal critics who question the credibility of his tales, and after reading 'Ice' and 'The Incredible Voyage', I could understand why. My personal experience of Tristan Jones was not so much about the legendary author and sailor who spent almost his entire life at sea, but more about a crippled old man that somehow managed to leave an indelible legacy on a nation. Truly amazing!

WAIT

There was a delay of another five days for the alternator to arrive from Bangkok. Then, after fitting it we discovered that the drive pulleys were different, so none of the belts we had on board fitted the pullies. We had to find new belts. In the meantime, when we pulled Scallywag up to the fuelling jetty, we discovered that after filling our diesel tanks, we only had a 600-kilometer cruising range, more fuel containers were needed. We also filled up our two main freshwater tanks ready for the next leg of our voyage. Then another problem occurred. One of our tanks was an under-floor bladder-type bilge tank, which split when we filled it fully for the first time, flooding the bilges with fresh water. It was impossible to find another suitable tank in Phuket, so we had to have four extra freshwater containers lashed on deck as well as all the extra diesel fuel and petrol for the gen set.

The extreme tropical heat and humidity seemed to make each day slide by in slow motion. We ended up spending thirteen days altogether in Phuket, eventually departing on the 10th of Sept. In the meantime, we made a few new friends locally, and after being invited for a meal or two, I discovered the unforgettable taste of home-prepared Thai cooking. I have never had the same food experience from any Thai restaurant since. Mr Jit kept inviting us to parties with a bunch of single ladies floating around. I tried a couple of times to explain to him, that we were not rich yachties looking for girls. I was absolutely convinced by then that he was a very polite pimp on the side. I had a dance and a squeeze but no real money for the girls. Robin and I just bought them a few drinks.

ISA LEA

For days, no one seemed to be aboard our neighbour's yacht, Isa Lea. Then a surprise. When we returned to Scallywag, ten cartons of beer had been left in the cockpit with a thank-you note attached to one of them. We met the owner, Rick, and his daughter the next morning. Rick invited us on board for a coffee and told us he had sailed in single-handed, dropped the anchor, thought his boat was secure, went ashore, and then booked into a hotel in Phuket. Rick had pre-arranged to meet his daughter there. She was flying in to join him that night. After booking into his hotel, Rick had slipped in his bathroom, hitting his head on a tiled floor, leaving him concussed. Everyone was concerned when his daughter arrived later that night, and the staff couldn't raise him. She went up to the room with the staff and found her dad on the floor, semiconscious. Rick spent the next day in the hospital. When they finally got back to their boat a couple of days later, he discovered Robin's note. All's well that ends well, and Robin was over the moon with all our extra beer supplies. Ten cartons of beer take up a lot of room on a small yacht, and the only space we had left was in the shower. Priorities prevail, so we had a bucket wash for a while.

The day before we left Ao Chalong Bay, Robin caught up with Tristan Jones again at the lighthouse bar. Robin told him we were getting ready to leave and that I was a fan of Tristan's work, so Tristan gave Robin an uncorrected proof copy of his book 'Somewhere East of Suez" and signed it to me personally. Special!!

LEAVING PHUKET

8:00pm and Phuket's lights faded astern as we motored west, the sea flat as a millpond. The northern tip of Sumatra was next. This passage would take us further north with, hopefully, less ocean traffic. The last couple of weeks had been amazing. I felt so lucky, but now I was happy to be back out to sea again. Earlier in the day, we were about to drop off our Thai ensign onto Tristan's boat when we spotted him rowing out alone to his 40-foot catamaran. We watched on with interest as he made his way to his boat. When he arrived, he attached his dinghy to the davits between the two hulls at the stern; where he had another davit rigged on the deck to which he attached himself. I had to smile in admiration when he hauled himself out of the dinghy with the wheelchair still attached to his person. Then he swung himself and the wheelchair over and onto the deck. His catamaran was fitted out with hand holds around the central accommodation area and a track around the wheelhouse that Tristan could manage in his wheelchair. What a guy, 70 years old, no legs, and still sailing a 40-foot catamaran. We motored over to say hello. Tristan was happy to see us as we pulled alongside. We dropped off our Thai ensign to him, and I thanked him for the book. He thanked us for the flag and wished us a safe passage. I heard Tristan died the following year after a wonderful, rich, and highly unusual life.

SUMATRAN KNOCKDOWN

Apart from all the usual day-to-day problems, a couple of incidents stuck in my mind on our way to Cocos. Sailing double-handed for thousands of miles was never going to be easy. Our course over the top of Sumatra and through the Rondo passage was similar to our previous route on Snizort. I was off watch and half asleep around 11:00 am. We were only a few miles east of Rondo Island when I heard Robin yelling for help. Scallywag suddenly healed hard over as I went to get out of my bunk. I thought maybe we had hit something. Then I heard the howl of the wind. Robin screamed out, "JJ!" I shouted, "OK, hang on a second, I'm coming." By this time, the roar from the wind sounded like an express train. I should have put on some safety gear, but Robin sounded desperate; that's what happens under pressure! The rest of this yarn is probably best told in Robin's own words.

"All capital shipping on the Singapore route is supposed to pass north of Rondo Island. Unfortunately, very few do so. Into this same narrow passage, along with the fishing fleet, coastal boats, and ferries, include one small yacht, Scallywag. We are sailing close hauled into the westerly trades. I'm at the helm and have just done three rather busy hours avoiding all sorts of shipping. I can see a black Sumatran squall line coming fast from the west, and we need to reduce sail immediately. I shouted down to JJ, who was off watch in his bunk, and told him we must reef now, urgent! I had a fishing boat crossing our

bow, and at the same time, I had to bear away from him, which put us into the direct path of a container ship travelling east. As I luffed up to clear the oncoming ship, I could see the Sumatran was nearly on top of us. I screamed at JJ as the squall hit us while he was still getting his gear on. He then casually stuck his head out of the hatch, saw my problem with the main, and slowly crawled his way forward while I fought with the helm, 40 knots and white water over the deck as JJ reached the main sheet, a 50-knot blast of wind hit us and nearly knocked Scallywag flat, laying the mast over almost parallel to the sea. JJ just managed to release the main sheet but was now hanging on to the mast chest deep in whitewater. With the pressure off, the main Scallywag quickly righted herself and dragged JJ out of the sea. The squall line passed over us and turned into a howling storm that lasted for half an hour or more. The passing container ship sheltered us from the prevailing wind for a few minutes, and we managed to put a reef in the main. Where the fishing boats went, I don't know. All I could see were two more container ships bearing down on us, the second appearing to be overtaking the first. Time to set a course south and get the hell out of the Rondo traffic. I was in a black mood by the time my watch was over. Then the sun came out; the wind dropped to a pleasant 15 knots. JJ had dried off in time for his watch and had a leisurely sail in perfect conditions, clear of all the traffic on our new heading south-southwest towards Cocos Keeling Islands.
Robin."

BLACKWATER

The stress of the last few days was over. Ache and the top of Sumatra were now behind us. 4 am I was back on the dog watch. Above me the Milky Way is a waterfall of stars reflecting endlessly ahead on a mirror-flat sea. The moment vanished when the acrid smell of raw sewerage filled the air. We were obviously following in the wake of a capital ship that was pumping out it's bilge tanks. It was still sometime before dawn but when first light arrived, the sea's surface had brown oily patches all around us with bits of plastic and rubbish floating by. The air around us stank for hours until we managed to get upwind. I have a gut feeling that most capital ships dump their black water in the sea under the cover of night. We pushed further South, keeping clear of the Banda Aceh coast. There was a string of reefs and islands that ran for 800 nautical miles down the back of the west coast of Sumatra from Aceh to the South of the equator, similar to the Great Barrier Reef, so for this passage, Robin set our course closer to the coast, where we hoped to pick up more favourable winds. There was also a lot of traffic. At times it was very busy, with hundreds of local fishing boats around us. I decided to set out my fishing gear. I had a couple of hits when I thought I'd hooked something big. My 120k gear stretched out beyond breaking point and snapped off. Robin thought I had foul-hooked a semi-submerged teak log or something similar. Luckily, we didn't hit it. We could have lost our keel - an instant capsize. Teak logs regularly fell off the deck of coastal traders in these parts and could weigh many tonnes, and often lurked just below the surface.

PIRATES?

Another grey dawn, and we were motoring at four or five knots with no wind, as usual. The sea was again an oily flat calm when two fishing boats came up behind us. At that moment, I was sitting head down in the centre cockpit, bent over, trying to sort out some tangled fishing gear. I had my Sony Walkman music and headphones on, so initially, I didn't hear them as they approached, but I felt the vibrations through the hull from their exhaust. Maybe they couldn't see me bent over as they passed close to either side of Scallywag. Still, when I did look up, I was shocked to see that the two boats were slowing down and closing together in front of me, leaving me nowhere to go. Oh ****! I knocked off our autopilot and spun the wheel hard over to starboard. At the same time, I shouted down to Robin that we had company and to get up on deck NOW! When I looked over my shoulder, I could see one of the crew members on the rear deck of the fishing boat checking out Scallywag through his binoculars. Then Robin popped up with his hat on, said "Morning JJ," and climbed out of the cockpit and onto the coach roof, then hung on to the mast for a better look. He is a big imposing-looking bloke, and remember, most of the Indonesian fishermen are about 5 feet nothing. We both waved to them, then I ducked down below and picked up the Minolta. When I returned to the cockpit, they could see I was taking shots of their boats. They quickly increased speed and waved back to us as they disappeared out of sight. Maybe they thought Scallywag was abandoned, or they were just having a bit of fun, trying to scare us, who knows, but it made me feel uneasy. Robin reckoned it was time for us to change course to a new heading south-south-west out to sea, away from the Sumatran coast and across the Indian Ocean. Cocos Islands was our next stop

GETTING THERE

Fortunately, they were the only incidents that caused any real concern on our way to Cocos. Days later, my second attempt at swimming over the equator was not to be. Squally weather ended that idea. Scallywag sailed over the line on the 18th of September at 1700 hours. She wasn't a quick boat and couldn't point very high into the wind, but she handled the ocean well. We did a lot of motor sailing to make better time south and keep the batteries charged. That was another problem we had to deal with. When we left Phuket, our electrics were supposed to be all fixed up, but we were getting flat batteries way too soon when we used the autopilot, even for short periods. Only later, after we arrived in Cocos, did we discover that the solar panels were discharging at night, and the voltage regulator was again on its way out. Reaching Cocos took the two of us another 8 days of hard sailing. Friends have asked me, "Didn't you ever get bored at sea with nothing to do all day?" Rarely, but why does anyone get into the delivery game anyway? Certainly not for the money, and then there are the inevitable delays and breakdowns. As some deliveries ended, I swore never again, but given time, the bad memories quickly fade, and another tempting adventure beckons. Ocean sailing can be an unforgettable experience, probably best described as you just have to be there. Some boat owners are under the delusion that the delivery crew will take their boat for a joyride. The truth is, it's a tough job and a real challenge. The idea of taking a boat for a little detour somewhere wouldn't come into our thinking - it's hard enough just getting a boat from A to B.

As the days slid by, I was trying to get a handle on celestial navigation and how to use a sextant, a dying art. It was interesting shooting noon sights, but I was making slow progress with the Almanack calendar and sight reduction tables. I finished reading Tristan's book 'Somewhere East of Suez' uncorrected proof copy. It was a great read. There were heaps of passages in the book that I'm sure would never have made the final copy. There were lots of colourful expletives regarding his book sponsors not being able to get funds and gear to him in some of the remotest locations of the globe.

MAN OVERBOARD

I was behind the helm, daydreaming in the middle of the afternoon, when Robin appeared in the cockpit with an empty beer carton in his hand and threw it over the side. "That's me. I've just fallen in, come and get me, or I'm dead." This took me totally by surprise. I had heard about this exercise but never actually practised it. My immediate reaction was to hit the 'man overboard' function on the GPS and then go about, tack through the wind and sail a reverse course. Doing this alone meant changing the jib sheets and resetting the sails. Robin stopped me; he said, "Can you still see me?" I had been trying to keep an eye on the beer box while going about. I looked back over Scallywag's stern. Relocating the floating box took me a few seconds or so, and to start with, I was looking totally in the wrong direction. The box was soon more than two wave tops behind us and getting harder to see all the time. Robin pointed out the problem. Lose track of a head in the water, and survival chances are not good. If Robin had really gone in, I would have thrown the danbuoy after him, but trying to turn Scallywag around and keep track of someone in the water by myself at the same time was nearly impossible. Additionally, I would need to start the engine, motor sail back past the man in the water, turn 180°, and try and stop the boat with the man close alongside, in the lee of the hull, sheltered from the wind and waves. Finally, haul the man in the water back on board. Not an easy task while alone!

Presuming I threw out the dan buoy first, I should have kept sailing in a straight line a while longer and thrown out whatever else I could find that floated to create a direct path back to the man in the water. At night, try to make a line of floating torches. I went through the whole exercise. Robin didn't say another word while I backtracked upwind. But the whole operation took too long. The beer box disappeared beneath the waves before I got there. There's a message here: don't fall in!

Some time ago, I was given the tip about carrying a personal radio, so when sailing offshore, I carry a small handheld ICOM VHF waterproof floating radio in my pocket. In the event of falling overboard, I could easily contact and direct any rescue vessel in the area directly back to me on VHF channel 16. They wouldn't even need to sight me. The radio also features a brilliant blue flashing LED light, which is particularly useful in the event of a night rescue. The personal EPIRBs that most solo and recreational fishermen use today are great, but think about the actual timeline. If you happen to fall overboard and then activate the personal beacon, that's it. No more contact until the Coast Guard or someone with a boat alerted by the system can spot your head in the water. Maybe hours in the sea. Hypothermia can set in after only a few minutes, depending on the water temperature. Other boats could pass close by without ever seeing you, just a head bobbing around in the open sea with no way to contact anyone. But a waterproof VHF radio has a range of around 20 kilometres, and a call on channel 16 can be picked up by the Coast Guard or anyone in listening range - a real lifesaver in a possibly fatal situation for a couple of hundred dollars.

COCOS MARK TWO

We were less than 10 kilometres north of the entrance to Direction Island around at 1600. There were a couple of frigate birds circling high overhead to greet us. We were so close, then a fresh breeze sprung up from the wrong direction and pushed us way out to the northwest of the island. By the time the wind eased off, it was getting dark and too late to try to make the moorings at night, so we stood off for another night at sea and waited till dawn. The new day brought us a favourable wind, and Scallywag sailed into the Port Refuge channel entrance and the Direction Island moorings at 0700. Seventeen days after leaving Phuket, we had only averaged around 70 miles a day. We were both totally stuffed, but once Scallywag was moored up to the quarantine buoy, we could relax. It felt so good just to stop and breathe, then lie down on a bed that was hardly moving. After an hour or so in the bunk, we were both feeling recharged and ready for breakfast.

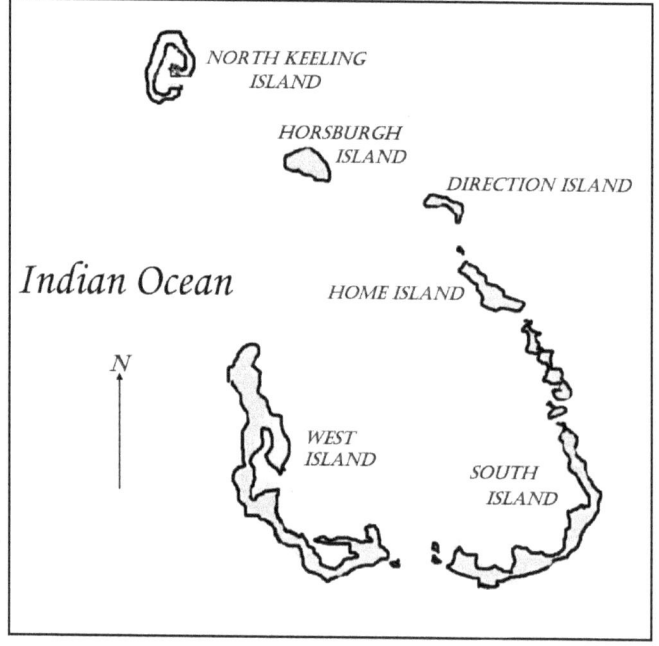

COCOS ISLANDS

Cocos was just a speck in the Indian Ocean, but what a magic destination. It felt great to be back after having left 13 months previously. The lagoon moorings were busy, full of visiting international yachts, charter boats, and yachts preparing for the next leg of their journey.

We needed to clear in, but first we made a quick call to Ashley on the radio phone to let him know we had made it to Cocos. Next, I attempted to contact customs on VHF channel 20. Calling every few minutes, hoping to get in touch with Dieter, my friend in customs, or the harbourmaster. I picked up other visiting yachts that were listening in, along with some background chatter, but nothing from customs or administration. After calling on and off for 30 minutes with no luck, Robin thought they were busy or out of the office. So, we decided to give Scallywag a scrub-up. Robin cleaned the topsides while I jumped into the crystal-clear water of the lagoon for a look below the waterline. It wasn't too bad, only a thin green gelatinous film had formed all over the hull. Just a gentle hand rub, and it was gone. Somehow it had managed to hang on through all the storms. We had also picked up a piece of fishing net wrapped around the rudder which was easily pulled off, but it would have slowed us down.

CHANNEL TWENTY TROUBLE

While I was paddling around Scallywag, Robin repeatedly tried to raise customs but still had no luck. Then I had an idea. "What if I swim ashore and call West Island from the free phone box on the beach?" A Victorian-era English-style phone box was just off the beach beside the jetty. It had a bright red cast iron frame with little square windows. No doubt it would have been imported years ago by the Clunnies-Ross family. The phone box was for the benefit of visiting yachts, enabling them to contact customs. Robin said, "Maybe that's not such a good idea, JJ, we're not really supposed to leave the boat till we clear in." I thought if I could raise Dieter, he would understand, and there wouldn't be a major problem. So, I had a leisurely 50-metre swim to the beach. Legs felt like rubber as I walked to the phone box. It looked totally out of place, bright red, and sitting under the palm trees like Doctor Who had just landed.

I opened the door and picked up the receiver. The words 'That's when the **** hit the fan' came to mind seconds later. When I first said hello, it was not Deiter or the harbour master who answered the phone. Instead, I was speaking to the new Cocos Island police Sergeant. I tried to tell him I swam ashore after we couldn't raise anyone on channel 20, but he didn't want to listen to my story and was not a happy man. He wanted to know who had given me permission to leave the Scallywag and also inquired about the name of the boat's skipper. I was then instructed to return to Scallywag immediately. He told me I could potentially face arrest when he came over in the customs vessel. Oops! I swam straight back to the Scallywag and shared the not so good news with Robin. I think that's about as near as I have seen Robin coming to losing it. "After all my visits to Cocos with a clean custom sheet, now I'll bet I'm going to be on the to-watch list, brilliant JJ!" It was a stupid idea, but what's done is done.

After an anxious wait, the Custom's vessel pulled alongside. I was relieved to see Dieter with the Police Sergeant. It was like being a school kid getting a bollocking by the headmaster. We could only listen to the inevitable. "You are professionals and obviously know the correct procedure. I can't think of any reason why you both should not be held fully accountable." I decided it was better not to say anything. Robin humbly apologised and accepted full responsibility for my impatience. The Sergeant then noted Robin's clean record from previous visits to Cocos. Maybe a little intervention there from Dieter, who stood back and didn't say a word through the whole conversation, would have helped. The Sergeant finished with something like, "There won't be another warning! Got it?" Robin and I nodded our heads in unison.

Then we had the usual customs declarations and handed over all our perishable stuff in a black plastic bag. By this time, it was 11 am. After five hours, we were finally cleared in. The Sergeant and Deiter went to reboard their Customs boat when Deiter turned to me and said, "There is a surprise for you two at the post office." Neither of us had any idea what he was talking about. Once the Customs boat left, our next job was to move Scallywag off the quarantine buoy and drop anchor in the lagoon. This time at a safe distance from other boats!

We had a long list of things we needed to do and fix, which meant visiting West Island, where all the facilities, shopping, and administration were located. First, we needed to inflate our Avon rubber dinghy and rig the outboard. Nothing much was said while we were launching the rubber duck, but Dieter's words were running around in my head. A surprise?!

The distance across the lagoon to West Island was about 13 kilometres, a long way in a little two-man rubber duck. But, just under 2 kilometres south of our position was Home Island - the nearest inhabited island. Once there, we can catch the inter-island ferry to West Island. Home Island is part of the ring of outer coral reefs that surround Cocos. The island is roughly 3 kilometres long overall and has a T-bone steak shape, mostly around 60 metres wide at the northern end, then thickens to nearly a kilometre at the southern end.

There is a village on Home Island where an ex-Malay community of around 450 people lived as Australian citizens. At the island's southern end, on a point of land, stands the Clunnies-Ross mansion, 'Oceania House'. This very unusual mix of two cultures have coexisted side by side on this tiny island for almost 150 years. We knew one of the local Malay guys. Abadin, who had previously helped us with Snizort, was a good marine mechanic and very much in demand. As soon as we landed on Home Island and pulled the Avon up the beach, we tracked Abadin down to his house in the village. Abadin welcomed us like an old friend, but told Robin he could not check out Scallywag immediately, as he was just too busy. We would have to wait a day or two. Nearly every other yacht that arrives at Cocos needs help from a good marine mechanic, so securing Abadin's help was our first priority.

As we were leaving his house, Robin said. "There's just one thing we need to remember JJ, Abadin is a devout Muslim and needs to pray facing Mecca several times a day. He also takes a little while to prepare his food and likes to have a nice, friendly little chat, so patience will be needed as progress can be painfully s-l-o-w." We overheard one of the ex-pats in the administration say, "Cocos time turns frustration into fascination."

THE STAMPS

After our meeting, we headed to the Home Island town jetty and waited for the ferry. Watching the R.J. Hawk pull up alongside gave me a flashback. For the last year, it felt like someone else was controlling my life while I was just an observer looking on. Little did I know fate was about to throw in another strange twist. Then we were all aboard, joined by several locals from the village with their kids, big smiles on their faces when some of them recognised us from our previous disaster. It felt warm and friendly to be back on Cocos. The trip across the lagoon to West Island took less than 20 minutes. Once we were moored, Robin and I stepped ashore. Several vehicles were parked around the jetty area, left with keys in the ignition, available for anyone's use. That might sound a bit strange, but the road from the jetty into the main town area was the only sealed road on West Island and less than 3 kilometres long. You couldn't steal a vehicle if you tried. There was nowhere to go and sharing keeps the number of vehicles on the island to a minimum. So, we all piled onto the back of a flatbed utility with some of the locals for a very short drive into town.

Once we arrived, Robin wanted to head straight over to the Customs building that housed the only place where you could get a cold beer. I was more curious to check out the 'surprise' at the post office. So, I said I'd catch him later at the bar. When I first walked into the post office, I had no idea what I was looking for. Robin said he thought Ashley had probably shipped something up for Scallywag. As I went to ask about the mail, I spotted the latest release of Cocos Island stamps on the wall behind the counter, a series of three stamps, all relating to our rescue, and a first-day edition envelope set. I was blown away, but then I couldn't figure out why. We were only in the dinghy for a couple of days, and it was a successful rescue. There were no casualties. To my way of thinking, the rescue was hardly worth commemorating with a stamp series.

I asked the lady working there how long the stamps had been available. She said, "Oh, just last month on the 17th of August.". Wow! I shook my head in disbelief. What a bizarre coincidence. The 17th of August was my daughter Claire's birthday! I picked up one of the first-day edition envelopes. The circular seal read 'August 17, 1993.' I had another puzzling thought. This is all really strange. Why weren't we informed that a stamp series commemorating our rescue was happening? After all, weren't we what the rescue was all about? Surely, we should have been at least informed or contacted by someone. The lady at the post office was quite surprised when I told her who I was and that we were the guys on the stamps. Like me, she was also a little incredulous as to why we had not been kept in the loop. Let's face it, most people are dead before they get their image on a stamp.

Whatever the reason, this was one of those life-changing events. I had a light bulb moment. I was at the post office on Cocos Island with my own Cocos Islands stamps and personal envelopes, so I sat down and wrote a bunch of letters to Mum, Christina, and other members of my family. I then placed the letters in the first-day edition envelopes and posted them off. I'm sure that must have been a philatelic world first. I bought another couple of sets to take home. It was time to head back to the Customs building, catch up with Robin and share the good news. Robin was downing his third beer and wondering what was taking me so long to pick up the mail.

FIRST DAY EDITION STAMPS

When I told Robin about the stamps, he was just as surprised as I had been. We returned to the post office, where Robin bought a couple of souvenir sets. Then, we decided to book into one of the motel-style cabins on the Island and take a break from Scallywag for the night.

After half an hour and hot shower, we were making our way back to the bar when we ran into Dieter, who was heading in the same direction. We all settled in for an ale or two. I had lots of questions I wanted to ask regarding the stamps, but Dieter wanted to clear up the situation regarding our communication problem earlier and the Customs screw-up. I just wanted to forget the whole thing. It was simply a stupid mistake on my part. But Dieter wanted to explain the reason for the entire episode. He told us we could not raise anyone in customs on VHF channel 20 because the Indonesian fishing fleet had been venturing further out towards Cocos recently, and they were using channel 20 for all their boat-to-boat communications. That's all ok if you log in on channel 20 and then switch to another channel for a conversation, but Dieter said the whole fleet was talking over each other, jamming the frequency. The high-power receiver in the Customs Office had been temporarily moved to another room because of the endless din and Indonesian chatter. No one heard my call when we first made Coco. No one was listening. What if our call had been an SOS? Dieter said that after our incident, the receiver would probably be moved back into the main office, and they would just have to put up with all the Indonesian crap. This was possibly the reason the Sergeant was so pissed off with us, but I didn't want to take it any further. Hearing that I didn't feel so bad about the whole incident. Our conversation then turned to the stamps. Dieter didn't claim to know all the answers, but he did say, "It looked like it all came down to politics and money. Not really focused on you guys at all. "

Our rescue vessel, the R.J. Hawke, was built in West Australia for around one and a half million dollars, a bargain in today's market, but at the time there was a lot of political opposition which consisted of the usual complaints about the waste of public money spent on a tiny island that no one had even heard of, etcetera. So, when we were rescued only weeks after the R.J. Hawke was launched, the Labour government, led by our then prime minister R. J. Hawke, probably used the media to promote the rescue as a good news event. An election was also approaching, and our rescue proved to the media and the opposition that the money was very well spent. My guess is some government bright spark came up with the idea for the Cocos Island stamp series, celebrating our rescue. One of the stamps features the R.J. Hawke, and I think that's all good stuff, great PR, they just forgot one tiny little detail: US! If we hadn't sailed back into Cocos when we did none of us would have ever known about the stamps. Eventually another set of Cocos stamps would have been published, and that would have been the end of it. Unless someone notified us, we would have been none the wiser.

It was great to have a night ashore. My first job in the morning was to review our shopping list and then restock the boat. I headed off to the one and only store on West Island, where I discovered just a few basics were left on the shelves. We had literally missed the boat. It turned out getting anything on the island was a bit of a raffle. A State Ship visited the islands once a month with fresh goods and supplies from the Australian mainland. For a couple of days after the ship came in the local shop resembled one of those scenes from a Christmas sale at a big city department store...yachties, admin staff, tourists, and locals, along with the Malay community, squabbled amongst themselves over the limited supplies. Quite funny, really. People tend to hoard, so some items, thankfully, had to be rationed. When I asked at the store when the next supply boat would arrive, they told me it wasn't due until the 11th of October - another two weeks. Nothing was fresh. There was nothing much of anything, really. It looked like we were stuck on Cocos, living on whatever we could scrounge until the next supply boat arrived.

Neither of us was too unhappy about being stuck on Cocos for a couple of weeks, and Scallywag had several problems that needed fixing. However, as it worked out, we were still having major electrical problems by the time the State Ship arrived. Our parts, flown up from Perth, didn't arrive till the 9th. Abidin, our mechanic, said he was not up on electrics, so he put us in touch with Mark, a marine electrician, to sort out Scallywag's power problems. Mark was based on West Island, 13kms away from our moorings, so just getting him to the boat was a challenge. Everyone was flat out, but progress happens at a snail's pace. When Mark finally got to Scallywag, he discovered that somebody had got it wrong and the solar panels were discharging at night. Second-hand parts had to be scrounged from what was available at Cocos. Mark also gave us the bad news that Scallywag's starter motor was on the way out. Then our 5hp outboard kept breaking down, a pain in the arse that occasionally meant rowing the two kilometres to Home Island with our rubber duck to catch the ferry.

OCEANIA HOUSE

One afternoon, while we were on Home Island waiting for the ferry, Robin and I decided to visit the Clunnies-Ross Mansion, Oceania House, and say hello to John Clunnies-Ross if he was at home. It was just a short 10-minute walk to the other end of the island from the Malay village. As we walked past the outer perimeter wall, there was an immediate feeling that something was wrong. What a difference a year or so makes! I couldn't believe what I was seeing. The beautiful old, gleaming white mansion was deserted and appeared dilapidated, with weeds growing around the lower windows and the front door. A curtain of cobwebs covered the windows. I tried the glass-panelled front door. It wasn't even locked and simply pushed open through the overgrowth. It was hard to believe what I was looking at when I walked in through the dusty, deserted main hall and into the chess room. The fantastic ancient library, including all the first-day editions, had been stripped from the teak-panelled shelves. Hundreds of books were left in a pile on the floor. I could see visible green mould on some of the leather-bound covers. Robin spotted a giant leopard cowrie shell lying on the floor among the books. He said, "Do you recognise it?" I picked the shell up. The last time I remember seeing the extremely rare shell, it was being used as a paperweight on the desk of John Clunnies-Ross. What had happened?

Immediately after the Australian government took over control of the strategically important islands from the British government in 1955, they wanted the Clunnies-Ross influence out of Cocos and out of his mansion, Oceania House on Home Island. His family was a powerful presence on the island, representing a fiefdom by royal decree. The press originally described Cecil Clunnies-Ross senior as "The benevolent King of Cocos." John told me his father had even received Queen Elizabeth and Prince Philip on a royal visit to the islands in 1954. John relived the story of his dad getting into a panic when the queen's representatives informed him that the toilets at Oceania House were not up to royal standards, and then in double quick time, had to build a suitable loo for Her Majesty. The cost was around $15.000 - a fortune for the family to spend at that time. According to John, the royal tush never needed to use the facility while visiting Cocos anyway! John told us that the royal entourage always kept a personal leather toilet seat slipover handy for Her Majesty in case of emergency.

The Australian Government had initially offered to buy the Clunnies-Ross family out, but when he refused, they threatened to annex his property. He then won a

High Court appeal, as there were no legal grounds to evict him, but still, the Australian government pressed him. John's father, Cecil, was accused of not educating the Malay community in his care, keeping them illiterate, but the truth was very different. Clunnies Ross had built a small school for the Malay villages, but education in English was not mandatory. John respected the predominantly Muslim culture, which had an Islamic education system all their own. When the initial deal fell through, Tom Uren, the then Australian foreign minister, later reneged on an earlier agreement that would see control of the island group relinquished to the Australian Government by the Clunnies-Ross family but let them still retain Oceania House, their ancestral home. But that was not to be. The government wanted the Clunnies-Ross influence on Cocos to be finished, eventually pressuring the family into selling all their islands and family home, with bankruptcy looming, for only $6.25 million.

Clunnies-Ross senior had previously invested heavily in purchasing a medium-sized coastal trading ship, which was to be manned by the village guys from Home Island. His idea was to complement the State Shipping Service, returning with much-needed supplies for Cocos and stopping at other ports en route, at the same time giving the local village guys some experience and a start in the shipping industry. But his ship was refused entry into Australian ports due to technicalities regarding the way the crew would be paid, apparently not up to the Australian maritime seaman's award. I suspect this final blow pushed him over the edge and into bankruptcy. Clunnies-Ross had no other choice but to accept the government's offer. They got rid of him in the end.

Once the Australian Government had total control of the island group, the Cocos-Malay community on Home Island were then given a referendum – a choice to become independent or integrate the island group with the

Australian mainland and become Australian citizens. Naturally, they chose to integrate. Interestingly, when one of the Clunnies-Ross line had died years earlier, his son and heir, George, who had married one of the Malay girls from the village, organised a democratic vote. The island community had to choose the ruler or Tuan (master). They overwhelmingly elected George Clunnies-Ross.

Integration with Australia meant that the island group was free of servitude and automatically became Australian citizens, entitled to social security and health care. They were no longer under the governing influence of the Clunnies-Ross family. I heard John was pressured into relinquishing control of his family home shortly after our previous visit with Snizort in 1992. At that time, we were unaware of the volatile political situation or that the Clunnies-Ross family were fighting for their very survival and island home. Years later, another ex-foreign minister of Australia, Andrew Peacock, said, "The family were very poorly treated by the Australian government of the day."

Once the Clunnies-Ross family had vacated Oceania House, the grounds and property were initially given over to the Malay village community. Did the Australian Government think the villagers on Home Island would continue to manage Oceania House as a heritage tourist attraction - the same as Clunnies-Ross had done - to generate much-needed tourist dollars? Wrong!

To the Malay villagers, Oceania House was a permanent reminder of 150 years of colonial rule in third world conditions. After speaking to some of the villagers, I had the impression they would have happily torn the house down brick by brick. When Robin and I came along that day it was painfully obvious the village locals had no interest in preserving any part of Oceania House. It seemed like they wanted nothing more to do with the place. Bad karma. Maybe they hoped it would just rot away.

Wandering around inside the old palatial home, I couldn't help but feel that history was being thrown in the garbage bin. Why wasn't the house at least locked up? Shouldn't the Australian Government have made the property heritage-listed and saved the book collection and the fabulous old mansion? We walked around the back of the property to where the extensive vegetable gardens were located. They had once provided enough vegies for the entire Home Island population and visiting tourists, but were now lost under waist-high weeds. I thought the villagers would have at least kept the veggie gardens going. But now they receive social security, so the necessity to be self-sufficient seemed to be no longer an issue. Island life!

We ran into John Clunnies-Ross Jr on West Island days later. What a comedown in living standards. The Australian Government had allocated him one of several weatherboard houses built alongside the landing strip on West Island - the same accommodation we were given after our rescue. John didn't seem at all bitter, and was still confident. He had moved on and now had other business ventures happening on Cocos. We had a couple of beers together. He was philosophical, believing all good things must come to an end. He was still positive, but did say that all the negative exposure in the press regarding his family's history was predictable once the Australian government decided to and push the Clunnies-Ross family out. Added to all this pressure, the responsibility of governing and providing for the education, housing, and welfare of the island Malay community after the copra trade dried up had become near financially impossible for his father, Cecil Clunnies-Ross senior. With very little income apart from tourism, the end was inevitable.

I felt so lucky that we had at least experienced a little of the former glory of Oceania House. Maybe our rescue celebration dinner party at the mansion was the last official big gig there before the Clunnies-Ross micro island empire ended. It was nice to look back and think we were part of that brief moment in the final chapter of Oceania House and the Clunnies Ross Cocos Islands family history.

SICK

Later that same week, I contracted Giardia from the water supply on Home Island, a microbial bug that causes terrible stomach cramps, nausea, sweating, and the runs. Living on board Scallywag was a nightmare. Doing anything was exhausting in the humid climate, especially trying to see the only doctor or get medication. Initially, I thought I had just picked up a tummy bug, but the headaches and fever were something else. The diagnosis and finally getting the pills took days, and by that time, I had lost a couple of kilos and was not in good shape at all. When I finally recovered after taking the medication, I did manage a few good days diving and fishing with the crew on Barnstormer, a beautiful 60ft cruising yacht that sailed into Cocos with a group of friends travelling around the world together. I still didn't feel wonderful, but Cocos isn't a bad place to recuperate. Our departure was planned for the 16th, but that morning we woke up to flat batteries. Another visit from the electrician Mark, who discovered that this time we had an earth leakage problem. After another four-hour battery recharge, we were told Scallywag was finally good to go. We hoped!

DAY ONE, MARK 2.

After three frustrating weeks on Cocos, we could finally leave Direction Island at 4 pm on the 18th. After a good send-off from our friends on Barnstormer, we headed through the channel and out into the open sea, very happy to be on our way again. At the same time, there was a bit of foreboding. Neither of us felt very confident about Scallywag's electrical system.

I set up the fishing gear before departure. Unfortunately, we didn't catch anything on the way out into deeper water and I didn't get another hit until we made the West Australian coast. The southeast trade winds blew consistently from 160 degrees south, which made our course almost identical to our previous passage on Snizort. At some point, we must have passed close to the wreck of Snizort, possibly thousands of meters below us, or somewhere close on top of the Murfield subsea mountain reef.

For the next nine days, we had to make it south, sailing as close to the wind as possible. This heading would eventually connect us with the Southern Ocean Westerly system. Sailing hard day and night for over a week, we were close-hauled and bashing into it most of the time. Occasionally there were days with little or no wind.

Robin came down with the runs one day after we left Cocos. I stayed on watch all that day with Robin flat out in his bunk. The voltage regulator system started to fail after only 2 days, which meant the batteries were overcharging while the engine was running and started to boil off. The new alternator was putting out too much juice and overloading the system. At night, we must have looked like a Christmas tree on water. We had to try to pull the excessive charge down, so we had all the cabin and navigation lights, the radio, and the sounder going. It wasn't that successful. The batteries were still overheating. The gas sniffers in the bilges became too hot to touch, automatically cutting off the gas supply to the stove. We made a manual gas bypass system from bits and pieces of copper pipe and rubber tubing so at least we could have a hot meal.

Every day there was something that needed fixing. As we sailed further and further south, the prevailing easterly system slowly dropped off, and we had a day or two of fluky, variable winds. At a position approximately 650 nautical miles SSW of Cocos on the 27th, we began to pick up the westerly trades. The westerlies meant we could finally change our heading and set our course east toward the West Australian coast. After our struggle with the elements since leaving Cocos, a following wind and sea felt like a holiday. However, reaching that position south, out in the middle of the Indian Ocean, had been anything but a holiday. Scallywag's heading since we left Cocos had been mostly west of south, which would eventually place us in a position close to 750 nautical miles off the West Australian coast. Truly in the middle of nowhere, many miles away from any of the shipping lanes and still 900 miles from our destination, Fremantle.

On the morning of the 5th day out from Cocos the starter motor failed. Hand cranking the turbo wasn't an option. That meant no main engine power. We needed to run the Volvo for a couple of hours in the morning and charge up the batteries for the autopilot and cool down the fridge at the same time. In the evening, we ran the engine for 3 or 4 hours to power the cabin and nav lights. With no engine it was back to manual helming - four hours on four off. Reading was by torchlight, and no more cold food or drinks. The worst part...warm beer! Our solar panel power was now reserved for the batteries, emergencies and the radio. We didn't have enough juice to leave our navigation lights on at night, so we notified the Australian Maritime Authority of our predicament by HF radio. Without navigation lights, no other vessels could see us at night - not that we ever saw another vessel after leaving Cocos anyway. Many frustrating hours were spent trying to fix Scallywag's starter motor, but it never went again.

MAYDAY
23ʳᴅ October Day 6

Every day we listened to the high seas weather forecast and at the same time monitored the dual-watch emergency VHF channel 16. There was a radio silent period for three minutes after the hour and another three minute silent period after the half hour just in case someone was in trouble and calling for help. We were about to turn off the radio after the weather forecast when we heard a static noise. It was a man's voice which kept breaking up. Then, we clearly heard him say he was being attacked somewhere off the coast of Bali. I could hear the fear in his voice when he took a deep breath and said, "They're coming!" Next, we heard him say something about his wife. There were intermittent words and radio static noises. We tried hard to listen but couldn't make out any other words. Bali was around 1000 miles northwest of our position, so we were getting radio skip. We did try to contact him once without success. Our batteries were too low, and our set wasn't powerful enough. Also, we had to consider that while we were trying to reach him, we could be jamming the frequency and possibly hindering a rescue effort for him. We listened in for a while but didn't hear anything. Eventually, we turned off the radio.

That incident put a real damper on the rest of the day. Neither of us said much. Robin contacted maritime authorities when we made shore, but they couldn't find any officially recorded incident.

It was another bad start to the day when Robin dislocated his finger, trapping it on a winch handle. Ouch! Then, the stainless-steel freshwater tank in the bow ruptured which was caused by the bow constantly rising and crashing into the sea. This triggered a bit of a panic.

We thought we were sinking again until we tasted the fresh water in the bilges. The tank had fractured halfway up on a weld. Once it had drained down to that level, it only leaked when we were healed hard over to port. Having water intermittently sloshing around in the bilges is a bit disconcerting and a pain in the arse. So, now our 80 litres of emergency water lashed on deck along with some bottled water had to get us home No more washing in fresh water. It was brush my teeth and swallow!

I picked up another bug from our water tank and felt rotten again. Lucky, I kept some pills from my previous infection. Neither of us felt good physically, and as we sailed further and further south, the warm trade winds turned slowly into the cold south-westerly winter pattern. The high point of our day was the phone schedule with Ashley. Once, I even managed a short conversation with Christina after Ashley transferred me through. We were still good! And I couldn't wait to get home.

Our run east into the West Australian coast started with a big following swell. The engine was dead. Now, we depended on our solar panels for all power needs. The Honda genset lashed on deck forward of the mast was sealed in a weatherproof box. I'm sure if we had tried to use it in that sea state it would have disappeared over the side in minutes. It was a different set-up to Snizort, where we had meters of open deck to stow a generator and two meters of freeboard.

With the prevailing wind and sea behind us, Scallywag romped along on a beam reach, logging over a hundred and ten miles a day on a very lumpy ocean with a big following swell. I wrote in the diary, 'God help anyone that gets seasick out here.' Scallywag felt like she was in a gigantic washing machine! Helming hour after hour, I got into the rhythm with the sea. I could feel every little twitch that Scallywag made as we ploughed through the ocean.

Later in the day after my watch, we spoke to Ashley and decided to change plans and make our first landfall at Geraldton, 300 kilometres north along the coast from Fremantle, our original destination. Geraldton, our closest coastal port, now lay east, 290 nautical miles directly ahead of us. As we approached the coast, we were aware of the Houtman Abrolhos Islands, a group of over a hundred islands and reefs running north-south about 60 kilometres off the coast of Geraldton which now lay directly ahead of us. We originally planned to sail south around the reefs and make our approach into Geraldton from the west, but the prevailing SW wind had other ideas for us and pushed Scallywag much further north as we closed the coast.

5th November diary entry: "No fireworks, but today, we put our clocks forward one and a half hours to local West Australian time. We also recorded our best days sailing, close to 140 nautical miles east in 24hrs. Scallywag's in the slot and has the bit between her teeth. Getting closer to the end of our journey, we could smell the land!"

ABROLHOS ISLANDS

The Abrolhos Islands were a treacherous, low-lying stretch of islands and reefs renowned for numerous shipwrecks. We made our approach at night from the north. North Island is at the top of the group and has a navigation light with a loom which should be seen from 7 miles. According to our GPS position, this light should have been clearly visible as our first sight of land but was very dim when it finally came into our field of view. This did not correspond with our GPS position, but we had to trust the GPS and our charts. Robin turned on the sounder, and the depth tallied with our navigation charts, so we were much closer to the reefs than we should have been. However, the light on North Island did not look very reassuring at all, more like a candle from our perspective. Fishermen told us later that the nav light was on a 5-meter tower covered with metal spines on top to keep the seagulls off. The trouble was there were so many seagulls trying to land on the tower in the daytime that some birds had been squashed down onto the spines, and then the other birds landed on top of them. The navigation light appeared dim because it was covered in dead birds and guano.

Other reefs run a little further north of North Island, so we gave it a much wider berth than originally planned. While Robin was on watch that night, he shouted down to me that there was a very strong smell of fuel, so I should not light the gas stove. I was about to start our evening meal when the acrid smell of fuel in the air hit me. I joined Robin in the cockpit. We figured a tanker must have left Geraldton heading north up the coast and was either leaking fuel or dumping it all over the surface. Robin reported the slick to Customs after we made port, and they told us that a tanker had been reported missing, some miles further up the coast from our position, off Norwegian Bay.

LANDFALL GERALDTON

Once clear of the Abrolhos Islands, Scallywag seemed to know her way home, and just for once, the gods were with us. We covered the last 80kms hardly touching the helm, and glided into the Geraldton Batavia marina at 6.30 pm with a gentle breeze behind us. Robin brought Scallywag alongside the T-head of the jetty. I jumped off with a mooring line in my hand, but when I landed on the solid surface, I couldn't stop and kept stepping forward till I stumbled over. My land legs were gone after 22 days at sea. I staggered back up like a drunk and took a turn on a bollard. Scallywag had made it back home to West Australia. We had logged a little over 3500 nautical miles since leaving Port Klang in Malaysia.

Once we were secure, we made a quick call to Ashley. He would be coming up immediately, and so was Christina after I invited her to join us for the last 200-mile leg of our journey back to Fremantle. When we checked in with Customs, they told us to stay on board until they arrived. When they did arrive, they treated us like drug smugglers. I thought they were going to pull Scallywag apart. I suppose when they checked our passports, it was clear that we were both frequent visitors to South East Asia (obviously very suspicious!) Once the officers were satisfied that we were not smugglers, they left, but not before warning us that we could expect to be boarded and thoroughly checked again by customs when we arrived in Fremantle.

Then I enjoyed my first shave and hot shower with fresh water in weeks. My skin felt like a greasy blanket. My hair was stiff and matted full of salt. Christina arrived with Ashley the following morning. It was so good to see her again. She looked gorgeous, but wasn't impressed with the state that Robin and I were in. She said we both looked really burned out. I needed a little TLC! Ashley got straight into fixing Scallywag's electrical system for the third time while we went shopping and restocked Scallywag's galley with a gourmet food selection and some local red wines for our final run home to Fremantle.

Having Christina on board for that last 200-mile leg was the beginning of many thousands of miles the three of us would sail together. Christina said that after we sailed out of Geraldton, she experienced what is best described as an epiphany. Some people love the sea, and some hate the experience. Christina fell in love with the whole thing from the word go. We all had a great time together, and the pressure was off. It was just a cruise along the coast to Fremantle. We caught beautiful fish along the way, washed down with some great Aussie wine.

CUSTOMS DOG

True to their word, the Customs guys were waiting for us when we tied up at the Fremantle Sailing Club a couple of days later. Then, to our surprise, the officers brought a German Shepherd along and went right through Scallywag again. One of the officers told Robin that the dog could smell drugs from two months ago. Robin replied that we hadn't been on board Scallywag for that length of time since leaving Port Klang in Malaysia. After the dog had a good sniff around the boat, we were finally cleared in and allowed to disembark.

A couple of pals I knew at the club wandered over to see what was going on. They were standing by on the jetty. "Hi JJ, good to see you back. What's happening?" They were curious and had come over when they saw the Customs Officers with their dog. I replied that we were undergoing a drug search. I mentioned the dog was able to detect the smell of drugs onboard from three months ago. My friend said, "Well Lassie's nose wasn't that good; the dog walked right past me, and I have a bag in my pocket with a bit of green in it!" We all cracked up laughing. I thought that was so funny. Christina said later, "It was the best way to end our first ocean voyage together."

MY DAY IN COURT

Years slip by, and the final chapter of my three-part story begins here. 1997. After eight years of litigation, sixty thousand dollars in legal fees, appeals, delays, and financial hardship, I finally dragged the hotel group into court, and we won. What a feeling! All my costs were paid. Hard to believe that the court case had taken nearly as long as I owned the bar. As I previously mentioned, my solicitor initially warned me that the entire process might take eighteen months. That was quite the understatement! But it was over, and for the first time in a long time, Christina and I could make some real plans for the future.

THE PROPOSAL

After winning the case, we decided to celebrate the victory with a holiday in the USA. While we were in Las Vegas, I proposed to Christina, only to receive a definite "No, you have to be joking. No way I'm getting married in the Pink Chapel!" However, two years later, it was Christina who proposed to me right after we were arrested at gunpoint off the coast of Bali by the Indonesian Navy during another delivery that went all wrong. While we were under arrest, Christina suddenly turned and said, "JJ, if we ever get out of this mess, let's get married." A very unusual proposal under very extraordinary circumstances. But that's a story for another day...

SOUTH AFRICA

Christina had gone to bed. I was watching the news in disbelief, like millions of others around the world, when the New York World Trade Centre Towers were hit. The attack on the World Trade Centre was particularly concerning to Christina and me as we had booked a holiday to South Africa just a couple of months earlier, shortly after our wedding.

We planned to visit my uncle Bill and his family, who lived north of Durban. After watching the attack, I thought this incident could be the trigger to start World War III. Thank God I was wrong!

Things settled down, and a month later, we boarded our SAA flight for Johannesburg, with a five-day stopover in Mauritius. This picturesque island is located 1000 kilometres east of Madagascar, in the middle of the Indian Ocean, and a favourite and little-known club med holiday destination for the well-heeled French. It is an amazing multi-cultural mix of people on an island paradise only 90 kilometres long - minus the Dodo bird! If you ever have the opportunity, go there.

EMPANGENI. BLACK MAGIC.

Another long flight from Mauritius, and we landed in Johannesburg to a warm welcome from my cousin Jill...Bill's daughter, who had driven up the day before. Once in her car, we faced a 230-kilometre drive east to Zululand, where she and Uncle Bill lived in the town of Empangeni, a few miles inland from Port Richards on the northeast coast of South Africa. This was my second visit to South Africa. I had previously spent six months on a working holiday in my twenties. In those days, Uncle Bill and his family lived in Durban having migrated there after the Second World War. I clearly remember the apartheid and public outcry during my time there - a period when Nelson Mandela was imprisoned on Robben Island, situated in a bay near Cape Town.

Cousin Jill now resided with her dad in a secure gated community after her husband passed away several years earlier. Neither Christina nor I had ever been in a gated community before. We immediately noticed the barbed wire atop the high walls surrounding the place when we drove into the compound, and everyone seemed to have a guard dog.

When we got out of the car, Jill said, "You knock, John." The front door opened. It was great to see Uncle Bill again after so many years. We gave each other a big hug, and then I introduced Christina. Sadly, Bill's wife Nancy, had also passed on since my last visit nearly 30 years earlier. Bill was still the same exuberant character I remembered from the 70s, and so happy to see us both. He was retired after spending his final working years as assistant harbour master at Port Richards, just a few miles away on the coast.

Empangeni turned out to be much bigger than I imagined, with a population of around 80,000. It was also the central business capital of the KwaZulu area, about 160 kilometres north of Durban. We soon settled in. Christina was thrilled when she discovered Cousin Jill owned a hairdressing salon in town. Bill introduced us to some of his friends living in the gated community. Then Jill took us for our first trip into downtown Empangeni for some shopping, which turned out to be a real eye-opener. After cruising around the town centre, Jill dropped Bill and me at a local bar, then took off with Christina to the hair salon. As we entered the foyer to the bar, there was a sign above the door: 'No weapons allowed inside'. Weapons had to be handed in and left with a doorman. Guns, knives, knuckle dusters, and steel bars numbered and locked in a glass case until you leave.

When Christina returned from the supermarket with Jill, she was quiet and not her usual bright self. I asked," You seem very quiet, what's wrong?" Christina said that there was a collage on the wall at the supermarket - photos of children who had been taken and kidnapped with appeals for help from parents. "Have you seen my little girl?" Jill tried to explain to us that the kidnappings had something to do with black magic and the AIDS HIV virus, but it all sounded too horrific. Little white girls were a prize. The area we were living in was called KwaZulu and was still very tribal. Black magic and witch doctors were immensely powerful and influential in this region. The witch doctors had laid the blame for the AIDS HIV virus that was spreading through the black community on white people.

Jill took us one Saturday morning to the Shebeen, a market with all the usual local crafts and fruit stalls, along with a bar selling 70% cane spirit. Then Jill pointed out a dark section at the rear of the market devoted to the black arts, selling all sorts of native animal body parts including gorilla's hands, teeth, elephant's feet, jaw bones and what looked like dried eyes. Unbelievable in this day and age.

Jill said her kids had grown up in Durban but ultimately decided to move back to Scotland with their families for security reasons. Jill did say, "It's the saddest thing. You will never see white kids playing out on the street here anymore." That was the first time Christina and I both experienced the uneasy feeling that comes with wondering if this trip might not have been such a good idea. Bill was full of stories of the old days and how some of our family had left Scotland way back in the 17th century, and that the Patersons were now scattered all over the planet. Then he mentioned that there was even a town in South Africa named Paterson, which lay hundreds of kilometres south near Port Elizabeth - apparently named after one of our long-lost relatives from Aberdeen. Bill suggested it could be something worth exploring. We could take a road trip south and discover South Africa.

Bill asked me what I had been doing with my life for the last few years, and our conversation eventually got around to the story of my rescue off the Cocos Islands and the commemorative stamps. He listened intently, and when I finished, he said, "John, I want you to listen while I tell you the complete story about what happened to your uncle Jack." He then told us the whole story, relating to his younger brother Jack's loss in the Atlantic in 1942 during World War II. Bill recalled the whole thing like it was yesterday. Even now, after all these years, he said, he still felt guilty for getting his kid brother Jack that fateful job on the SS Cerinthus. We drank and talked for hours. It was a night of family reminiscing.

Christina and I had booked a month for our South African holiday, so we had plenty of time to explore. The idea of driving down to Port Elizabeth was starting to sound fun. We could stop in Durban on the way and then follow the Garden Route south for about 800 kilometres along the coast, then cut across inland down to Port Elizabeth and check out this place called Paterson on the way. When I told Jill, we were planning to make the trip south, she suggested a friend who owned a car hire company. Being a friend of Jill's, instead of getting a generic box on wheels, we were upgraded to a hot silver Renault Megane coupe. When we first sat in the car, and I turned the ignition key, the doors all automatically locked, and the windows wound up. Quite the security feature!

Later that evening, after we drove the car home, one of Bill's friends took me to the side and said, "There are a few things you need to take into consideration before you two go anywhere." He then pointed out an article in the local newspaper. I hadn't really paid any attention to the newspapers up until then. It was a Saturday morning edition. Below the main story on the front page was a regular weekend guide and instructions on what to do if you are hijacked at a service station to avoid being shot. "Do not reach into your car. Avoid eye contact. No sudden moves. Do not put your hand inside your jacket, and always do as instructed."

Then Jill, who was listening in, warned us not to stop if a policeman tried to wave us down. She told us that since the beginning of the year, a number of local policemen in the area had been murdered on the way home, stabbed in the back just for their uniforms! She said if it's a real policeman, they will come after you with a car or a bike. I was advised to slow down but not completely stop at a stop sign, always be ready to take off if someone suddenly approaches your car, and never to drive around with the windows down. Another one of Bill's friends asked how I felt about taking a weapon along for safety, and he said he had a handgun I could borrow. That all sounded like anarchy to me.

What had happened to South Africa? It wasn't that bad in the apartheid era Africa that I left so long ago. The black population, as I remembered, were generally a happy bunch. I thought the political situation would have improved since the end of apartheid, not worsened After dinner, Bill brought Christina and me up to date with the current political situation as he saw it. According to Bill, since the end of apartheid, African kids have been receiving a proper education, and they are now discovering for the first time what their colonial rulers, both English and Dutch settlers, took away from them.

Before the end of apartheid, Bill said that black kids were not even taught Zulu or Bantu at school, their own native tongues, but only English and Afrikaans, they received no historical facts and very little information about their own history. Like most native or indigenous people around the world today, they had to depend on stories handed down through generations to learn the truth about their own culture and their perspective on the country's history. During the apartheid era, the only source of that information, as usual, was from their elders. I laughed when Bill told me that the main languages now taught in South African schools are English, Zulu, and Bantu. Afrikaans was no longer taught in public schools around Empangeni. That all sounded a bit like revenge to me.

Bill said, "There are a lot of angry young men out there, and you must also understand that the racial problems are not just between whites and blacks. There is also a lot of friction between Zulu, East Indians, and the Bantu people. At the same time, the majority of native African people just want to move on and forget about the past." He made an analogy, comparing South Africa to Australia. Bill asked me, "It's easy for Australians to criticise the apartheid policy. What if Australia had the same population imbalance as South Africa? Forty million native Aboriginal population to four million white people, life sure would be different in Australia under your democratic one-vote system! Yes?"

We sat around and talked all night. Bill thought our trip south would be OK if we stuck to the main roads and never travelled at night. He said, "The further south you go, the less likely you are to run into trouble." Then I got a laugh out of Bill when I asked what I thought was a relevant question. "Do I have to worry about wildlife on the road while driving south?' In Australia, we have to look out for kangaroos and emus on the country roads." Bill thought that was funny and said, "The only wildlife you have to worry about is on two legs! All the game and native animals are in reserves, or they'd get eaten!"

Before we committed to a long journey south, we decided to take a more local run in the Megane first. Christina had picked up a flyer in town for some hot springs called the Thangami Lodge and Hot Mineral Spa. So, a four-day round road trip was hurriedly organized. Our trip would take us through the 'Imfolosi Game Reserve', about 80 km north as the crow flies from Empangeni. It was a mountainous countryside full of ravines and gorges. According to our tourist guide, the 'Imfolosi Game Reserve' is the oldest one in South Africa, home to both black and white rhino, as well as a huge elephant population and big cats. The reserve covers nearly 1000 square kilometres, much bigger than I had imagined. Our road trip would be around 400 kilometres all up.

Personally, I wasn't feeling that confident about the whole thing, but Christina was attracted by the sound of the hot mineral springs. We planned to spend a day driving east-west through the game park, then stop at a town called Ulundi for the night on the other side of the reserve. The next day, we would drive on to the Thangami Hot Springs Lodge. The weather was looking great for our trip north to the reserve. Before we left Empangeni, with some apprehension, I pulled into a service station to fill up the Megane. Three young African guys came straight over to the car. I wasn't sure what was going to happen next. Initially, I was going to get out and check the tyre pressure myself, but one of the young guys signalled me to stay in the car. He was polite and told me that if I cleaned the car, I would be taking his job away. So, while we sat in the car, everything was checked for us. One guy filled the tank, another one washed the windscreen and checked the tyres, and then the third one popped the bonnet and checked my oil and water. Naturally, everyone expects to be paid, but that's how it goes. I didn't want to argue with anyone, so we just smiled and said "Thank you."

IMFOLOZI GAME RESERVE

The Megane was a buzz to drive on the highway. By mid-morning we reached the turn-off onto the R618, which took us to the park entrance, finally arriving at the Nyalarzi Gate at about 11 am. After we paid the ranger, a big Zulu guy, he asked us how long we intended to stay and if we needed directions to one of the park lodges. I think he was really surprised when I told him we were just going to drive straight across the park and then out through the Cengeni Gate on the west side. He shook his head and smiled, then handed me a brochure with a road map of the reserve.

The park roads were mainly unsealed and had a speed limit of 40kph. The total distance across the reserve was only around 60 kilometres, but what I didn't realise was that the reserve road followed the Black Imfolosi River, which snakes around all over the place, making the trip west more like 100 kilometres. As we made our way in, and after only a few kilometres into the park, the fantastic wild rocky gorges blew us away, a dense jungle with overhanging cliffs. The reason the road followed the river soon became obvious when a herd of black and white rhinos appeared ahead at an elbow in the river. They were still over a hundred meters from the road, and we stopped only for a few minutes. I really didn't think we had time to stay too long if we were going to get out of the reserve by 5 pm and make Ulundi before dark.

After that initial sighting of the rhino, the only other animal we saw for an hour or so was a giraffe, its head poking out of the trees, and that was quite a distance away. I could see that Christina was a bit disappointed. I guess we both thought that was it… no more African game. We passed a couple of hides situated next to water holes, but sitting for hours waiting for wildlife to appear was out of the question. It was approaching 4 pm, and we needed to keep moving as the west gate was still a few kms ahead of us. At the same time as we pushed on, a storm front was building up in the west and heading our way. The ominous black wall of cloud quickly grew and grew as we drove west. Eventually, it was right overhead. A brilliant flash of lightning was followed immediately by some of the loudest thunder I have ever heard. The car shook as we both said, "Oh shit!" together and less than a minute later, the rain started bucketing down. I had to slow to a crawl, and then Christina said, "JJ, look." Animals were appearing all over the place in the pouring rain.

THE ELEPHANT

I had to stop when wildebeests wandered onto the road in front of the car. A giraffe appeared with its calf, towering over us. The calf turned to stare at us with huge feminine eyes. Christina said, "Look at those eyelashes." There was no choice. We had to stop and sit there in the pouring rain and enjoy the passing parade. It was amazing. For a short while, it felt as though we were in the midst of the herd. The African game literally surrounded our car. The rain began to ease a little, and the windows were steaming up, so I wound my window down a few inches when Christina shouted, "JJ, the window!" I turned my head. It was so close. I could have touched it. I was looking up into the eye of an adult elephant, water dripping off its long brown eyelashes, standing right alongside our little car. It was an eyeball-to-eyeball moment. The elephant had not made a sound as it approached us. A four-ton wall of muscle and bone simply appeared beside the Megane, water streaming down its hide. It was really checking us out, looking down into the car. I just hoped it didn't decide to scratch itself or sit on us. We felt tiny next to this giant. The elephant only stayed 30 seconds or so, then slowly moved on, just as silently as it arrived, disappearing into the African bush. I looked across the car at Christina, and her face was beaming. I think we had both been holding our breath while the elephant was alongside the car.

The road ahead began to clear, and we moved slowly through the African wildlife. They were obviously enjoying the damp conditions, with gazelles leaping around us and grazing on the wet ground cover. We didn't see any big cats, but it was an unforgettable experience. We both felt privileged to have witnessed those incredible minutes in the rain. Considering we were only in the park for a few hours, the Imfolosi Game Reserve truly put on a display for us and more than met our expectations.

ULUNDI

We made the Cengeni gate with minutes to spare. The road west out of the reserve to Ulundi was sealed but in poor condition, with potholes and crumbling edges. According to my rough map, Ulundi was about 40 km ahead. The road ran over the open countryside for 20 minutes, then forked. I couldn't see a sign for Ulundi, so I stopped the car, got out for a look around, and discovered the remains of a steel post cut off just above ground level. (I was told later the locals remove the signs for building materials).

As both roads were heading west, I chose the road that looked in a bit better condition. By 6 pm, the light was fading fast, and we were still under the storm cloud, with occasional downpours and lightning. Only two other cars were sighted on the winding road since we had left the game park. Bill's words of advice kept running through my head: "Don't drive at night."

We had originally left Empangeni with a full tank of gas, giving us a range of around 500 kilometres, more than enough for our 180-kilometre day trip to Ulundi. My problem was that I had been in second and third gear most of the day, so the fuel gauge was below a quarter. I still couldn't get out of third and was unsure if we were even on the right road. When daylight was gone, it truly disappeared. Pitch black beyond the headlights, illuminating the wet road surface. Occasionally, when a lightning flash occurred, we could see native people moving in the rain and silhouetted cattle grazing by the roadside. I was getting a really uneasy feeling inside when Christina said, "This is crazy, we have to stop and ask somebody" We passed another guy standing at the roadside, holding what looked like a short spear. In my mind, stopping the car was the last thing I wanted to do, but the alternative was possibly running out of fuel at night in the middle of the Kwa Zulu bush with no phone cover. Not a good situation!

We drove past a couple walking together at the side of the road, and Christina said, "JJ, please, stop" After pulling to a halt, I backed up a little and wound down the window a few inches. They were just a teenage couple; the girl came over to my window, dripping wet but with a smile on her face. "Hello, mister" Her partner stayed back at the side of the road. I said, "Hi, please, can you help us? Is this the road to Ulundi?" "Oh yes," she pointed ahead, "Ulundi very soon." I thanked her, but then she asked if they could please have a lift to Ulundi with us as I was about to leave. That was a moment when I felt so embarrassed. I had to say no and apologise to her. On the small back seat of the Megane, there were two suitcases and a cool pack.

We both felt terrible leaving them there in the rain, but I simply didn't like the thought of them squeezed in behind us, and the young guy never approached the car the entire time we were stopped. I would have felt too vulnerable. Christina mentioned later that she could sense me starting to get tense and a bit wound up. She always manages to stay calm in these situations. We drove on, and I felt relieved that the pressure was gone. (Sooner or later, you just have to trust someone!). I couldn't help but wonder what the young couple thought of us for leaving them there in the rain after they had helped us. White people!

Less than a couple of kilometres later, as we crested the next hill, Ulundi spread below us like a twinkling jewel in the rain. A huge sigh of relief escaped from both of us. Twenty minutes later, we had checked into our hotel for the night, relaxing at the bar with a drink, the end of another crazy day. The town of Ulundi, we discovered, according to the hotel brochure, was both the last and the original capital of the Zulu kings.

Some of the following I read from the hotel brochure. Apparently, the Zulu empire and Ulundi came to an end after they fought the British in 1879; during the Anglo-Zulu wars. Lord Chelmsford, the commander of the British army in South Africa, was defeated and humiliated at the Battle of Isandlwana - the first time ever the British army had been defeated by natives. After the loss, Lord Chelmsford received orders to stand down and return to England, but he ignored the recall and regrouped a massive army to attack Ulundi, home of the Zulu king Cetshwayo. The Zulus had also lost a significant number of men at the recent battle at Rorke's Drift and, after observing the British army of thousands on the march, sent a runner to Chelmsford asking what terms he would accept. There would be no terms. Lord Chelmsford needed to avenge his honour before returning to the UK. And he had an ace up his sleeve. For the very first time, the British army would test a new and devastating weapon - the Gatling gun. When the battle commenced on the 4th of July 1879, the Zulus charged en masse in their usual manner, but this time, the overwhelming numbers ran into a hail of bullets from strategically placed Gatling guns. The slaughter continued for hours till there were virtually no Zulus left to fight with over a thousand bodies piled on top of each other. The British only lost fourteen men in the battle. Chelmsford's army then entered Ulundi and burned the Zulu capital to the ground. I heard, but I'm not sure if sure if it's true, that initially the British had no interest in fighting the warlike Zulus until gold was discovered north of the Black Imfolosi River. So, you could say we were on sacred ground. I suppose that piece of history would have contributed to the reluctance of white people to visit the colourful and very picturesque Natal region.

THANGAMI

Refreshed and ready to go after a good night's sleep and a great breakfast, we were told by our host that the Thangami Lodge was less than an hour's drive from Ulundi. Before we went anywhere, we needed to refuel the Megane, so we pulled into the service station and went through the same ritual with the local guys, who checked everything on the car. Then we were on our way to the open country. Huge valleys stretched endlessly ahead. It seemed like we were driving downhill forever, then uphill for kilometres. I thought we had stepped back in time when we came across a cow being slaughtered by a Zulu man at the side of the road. A line of colourfully dressed women waited with buckets to collect the blood and trays for the butchered meat. Other women were already walking away through the bush with the buckets balanced perfectly on their heads. We had heard the term subsistence farmer used in South Africa. Basically, native people live off the land in a shared community existence, same as it has always been.

There was very little traffic on our road, and most vehicles that we saw were all old 4-wheel drives. Then, a little later, we passed a truck half off the side of the road. As we passed, I took a quick look back in the rear vision mirror. There were two bullet holes in the shattered windscreen on the driver's side. Christina hadn't noticed the bullet holes, so I said nothing. I really didn't want to stop and see what had happened, so we pushed on. Our silver Megane must have looked like a fish out of water in that rugged country. Christina was questioning if we were still on the right road when we suddenly arrived at Thangamia. We drove through the spectacular gates built from a huge wooden framework of tree trunks, 5 meters high, decorated with massive elephant tusks. The brightly painted beams were covered with colourful flags, fluttered in the wind.

As soon as we entered through the open gate, the road led quickly downhill, about half a kilometre through the bush, into a collection of beautifully carved African-style timber and mud cabins. Each one had a small pool, and then there was a large building and a central administration area that we drove into. We had booked ahead, and when we arrived, a young lady stepped out to greet us. "Hi, welcome to Thangami". After we had registered, I asked our host what our cabin number was, and she started laughing. "Anyone you like, you guys are our first guests in a while. We don't get many tourists here anymore." I wanted to ask why. But thought that might have been an awkward question. Then Christina said, "It's beautiful, JJ. Let's wander around and then pick a cabin."

Our host pointed to a map of the place on the office wall. Thangami had been built on an area near the edge of a 40-metre-high cliff overlooking a rift valley with the Black Imfolosi River winding through it. So, we headed outside for a look, taking a short walk past the cabins. Once clear of the bush, the view along the valley from the cliff top was breathtaking. We could see for miles. Christina soon decided on one of the intricately carved cabins with its own hot pool. Then we made our way back to the administration building. When we told the receptionist which cabin we had chosen, she handed us the keys and then told us that there was also the 'Honeymoon Grotto' back in the cliff face, where the hot mineral water first bubbles out through the rock. "You're welcome to use it if you want to". I don't think I have ever seen Christina so happy.

After unpacking and settling into our accommodation, we picked up a couple of towels and followed the path leading into the honeymoon grotto. It was one of nature's little wonders, a natural cave in the rock face leading back to three bubbling hot pools, room enough for several people. We had it all to ourselves. The owners had installed soft lighting around the pools, with a couple of blue lights underwater. We got our kit off and jumped into the blood-heat water. It was just a magical experience, soaking in the heat at the end of the day. All our meals were booked at the lodge. It was excellent food, but we felt strange sitting in the dining room, being the only guests. The Afrikaner owners also lived at the lodge, which had been in their family for generations. Our receptionist, guide and waitress were very friendly and extremely curious about Australia. She told us that we were their very first Australian guests. She was a hive of information concerning the history of the Thangami hot springs.

SHAKA ZULU'S JACUZZI

The story goes that the locals had known about the hot mineral springs for generations. During the Zulu Wars of the late 19th century, after their fierce battles with the British army, Shaka Zulu and his warriors would return to Thangami and then disappear down the cliff for a bit of R and R in the hot springs. Christina and I had been bathing in Shaka Zulu's private spa!

Our two days at the resort flew past with a visit to the valley floor, which included mud pool baths followed by a dip in the Black Imfolosi...with a heavily armed guard standing by in case of crocodiles! Once back in our cabin for the night, I picked up an information booklet about the resort. When I turned to the back page, I was surprised to find a list of African game that could be shot for a price. I pointed this out to Christina. Crocs, Rhino, Warthogs and so on. At breakfast the following morning, I asked our hosts how that works in a game reserve. The answer was simple: there were a couple of native villages on the valley floor, and they could legally take a number of animals for bush meat. (Similar to the present situation in Australia with Aboriginal people). If a trophy hunter wanted to shoot big game, the villages would keep the bush meat and the quota of game taken would remain in balance. The proceeds helped to run the cash-strapped Thangami Lodge. I finally asked one of the staff why there were no other guests. Again, the AIDS HIV virus was to blame. White people feared being attacked in this area of KwaZulu because of all the rumours and negative publicity blaming whites for the virus. According to the media, gay white men had imported the AIDS HIV virus into South Africa from San Francisco (Fake news has been around for quite a while!)

They were still catering for local groups and school outings at Thangami, but their bread-and-butter tourist trade was gone. The virus had hit South Africa hard in so many ways. Maybe we had been lucky or just naïve, but we hadn't personally experienced any real negative interactions with black people. Some seemed to be a little wary of us, but mostly just helpful and friendly. The most significant difference I had noticed from my previous visit years ago was the way native people would now look down when approaching, totally the opposite of the 70s. Back in those days, I remember, there was always a big smile and a flash of gleaming white teeth when crossing paths with the locals. Christina said that she had the feeling that we were the aliens, the intruders and that we really didn't belong there. Our short stay at the Thangami Spa was at an end. After breakfast we loaded up the Megane, and following an enthusiastic farewell from our hosts we were back on the main highway driving south to Empangeni along with a brief collection of unforgettable African days.

THE ROAD TRIP

Even before we returned to Empangeni, serious plans for our road trip south to the town of Paterson had begun to crystallise. We got back to Empangeni well before dark, and it felt wonderful to have a home base to return to. Bill was his usual cheerful self, and after we recounted our adventure over a late meal, he gave us the "I told you everything would work out ok." Jill was a little more guarded. She felt we had been a bit lucky, and Christina had been in a very vulnerable situation; I should have done much more forward planning. Point taken.

DURBAN

Only a day or so was needed to get organised, and we were off again, waving goodbye to Jill and Bill. Durban was our next stop, 160 km south. There didn't appear to be any speed limits on the highway N2, so I wound up the Megane, and we had a great drive, hitting the outskirts of Durban before lunch. Tragically, like most South African cities at the time, Durban was surrounded by a ring of poverty. Thousands of people were just surviving in terrible conditions, desperate, hoping for a job, food, anything. We were aware that many people were dying with little or no health services, and the AIDS HIV virus was radiating through them like wildfire. Driving into the CBD was chaotic. We slowed to a crawl, trying to find somewhere to park our car. So much had changed. I hardly recognised any part of the city from my previous visit in the early 1970s.

During our drive south from Empangeni, I had been reminiscing with Christina about the similarities between the Durban seafront, known as the Golden Mile, with its hotels and beachfront entertainment, and how it reminded me of Surfers Paradise back in Queensland, Australia. The new reality was a big shock. I jokingly recalled that during the 70s, Durban was known as the white man's playground, but now it looked like spot the white guy.

Parking was impossible. Cars were banked three deep at the roadside, and while we were stopped, a young African guy came over. He could see we were trying to work out what to do next. I wound down the window. "Hey, Mista, look after the car for two rands." I joked to Christina that at least we will still have wheels on the car when we get back. Once we had located our hotel with off-street parking and the car was safe, Christina wanted to wander around downtown Durban and check out the markets. Again, I was a bit apprehensive as the black to white ratio was overwhelming. Anyway, we bravely decided to walk down into the main shopping area. Once outside our hotel and standing in the foyer, I was instantly reminded of Durban's unique, rich, earthy African aroma.

We made our way onto the street, and we were immediately swept along with a moving tide of people all bumping and jostling into each other. It was hot, noisy, and very colourful, with everyone talking loudly and thumping music radiating from minibuses packed with people, some hanging on the outside and shouting at their friends and other pedestrians. As we were making our way through the crowd, we nearly fell over a young woman sprawled out on the ground in a doorway, a baby in her arms. She and the baby appeared to be asleep or unconscious in the oppressive heat of the day, a plate for coins next to her. Earlier at our hotel, we had been warned about pickpockets, so shopping was a bit of a nerve-racking experience.

THE GOLDEN MILE

Christina needed to use the toilet. At 5ft 1", she looked tiny next to the Zulu woman, so I decided to stand guard outside the lady's toilet door for her. I got a few strange stares from other women passing by. Durban's seafront was still a few minutes' walk from the shopping centre in the CBD. This wasn't working out to be such a good idea, but after a claustrophobic struggle, we finally made it onto the beachfront esplanade and Claridge's Hotel. Claridge's bar overlooked the Golden Mile Beach and the esplanade. While we were making our way there, I had a flashback. Claridge's used to be my old stomping ground and a regular meeting place for the gang on a Friday night. The setting still looked spectacular and brought back vivid memories of party days from the '70s. We made our way to a table and soaked in the view. After drinks and a snack, I was relieved when Christina decided that would do it for the day. Enough reminiscing and touristy stuff. We both agreed to head back to our hotel. With the Durban seafront and the stunning ocean views now firmly locked into the memory bank, I booked a taxi, and 20 minutes later we were downing an ice-cold gin and tonic in the safety of our air-conditioned hotel bar. Bliss!

DURBAN THEATER

We had only booked in for an overnight stay at our hotel. While we were having a drink, Christina picked up a brochure for a local theatre production. She thought it sounded like some sort of musical singing, African dancing type thing (I can't remember the name of the production.) "JJ, we only have tonight; let's go and experience some live African music and theatre" "Okay, sounds like a good idea to me." We booked a couple of seats for the play through the hotel. After our evening meal, we decided to drive over to the theatre. It was only two blocks away, but we both felt it was too risky to walk at night. On the way there, we stopped next to an old African man folding cardboard boxes by the side of the road just to check if we were still going the right way. Christina opened the car door to ask the old man for directions. "Excuse me" was immediately met with. "Get back in your car, lady. It's not safe for people like you here." Christina closed the car door. We both thanked him for his concern and then he pointed around the corner to our destination, shaking his head.

There was a multi-story car park next door to the theatre. Once inside, we noticed that there were only a couple of other cars parked on the ground floor, which had dim lighting. Jill had warned me not to get straight out of the car in situations like this, so after stopping, I kept the engine running. We waited for a few seconds. Then Christina said, "Come on, JJ, this is silly; let's go." We locked up the car and quickly made our way outside.

The front of the theatre was well-lit. Cars were rolling up and dropping people at the door, all Africans. We entered the foyer and picked up a programme from the stands arranged around the foyer entrance. On the stands were many very faded black and white photos showing what appeared to be a concentration camp with thousands of black men looking through a barbed wire fence. I had an 'uh oh' moment; this was not going to be a musical comedy! We walked into the packed theatre and found our seats. I looked around but could only see one other white couple in the whole place.

We then sat through one of the most embarrassing ninety minutes of my life. The cast, mainly all native black women, were singing songs related to the end of the Boer War. Where are our men? We have been waiting for them to come home after ten long years of fighting. During the intermission, Christina went to the toilet. When she returned, she told me that she had overheard two young girls talking, saying that they had never been taught any of this history at school. I decided to read through the entire programme during the intermission.

Throughout the Boer War, both the British army and the Dutch farmers recruited thousands of young black men to assist them in their fight against their respective foes. Most of these men were employed behind the lines, performing menial tasks such as carrying ammunition or helping to prepare food, while some fought alongside the British and Dutch settlers on the front lines. These men were skilled in combat and in the use of various types of weapons. When the war finally concluded, the British victors, led by Lord Kitchener, faced a security dilemma. The 15,000 black men held in camps at the end of the war now posed a potential future threat. Then, according to my program, the British did the unthinkable. These men, the cream of African youth, were all repatriated with a package of food and blankets. But then came the ultimate treachery. My program read that before the British gave the blankets to the men, they first infected them with smallpox! The result, of course, was devastating.

When the women sang their last song, the theatre was initially quiet, then erupted into applause. We both felt like crawling under our seats. Minutes later, we left the theatre with the other patrons, some loudly and angrily discussing what they had just witnessed. We gingerly walked back into the poorly lit car park, our Megane alone, the only vehicle on that floor. It was a relief to get in and hear the reassuring self-locking doors click down. The short drive back to our hotel was made in silence. It was hard to believe that what we had seen and heard was true. It was quite depressing. I did try to find some historical recorded evidence of this gruesome story online, but all I could discover was a reference to the men returning home after the Boer War. As usual, the victors write the pages of history.

The next leg of our 1000 km trip south started with a little friendly advice from the concierge at our hotel. The following morning, after breakfast, as we were checking out, he asked me where we were headed. I told him we were driving south along the coast to Port Elizabeth. He asked if we had any accommodation booked and where we intended to stay. I said that we had nothing booked but planned to stay in B&B hotels that we had seen advertised in the local papers. He shook his head. "No, sir, that's not safe for you and your wife. You must stop in an Ultra-Station and make sure you check in before 5pm… that's when they lock the gates." I had never heard of the term Ultra Station before.

THE ROCK

Another full tank of gas, with the now usual pit crew in attendance, and the Megane was again cruising south down Highway N 2, along what is called the Hibiscus Coast…and for good reason. Once clear of the city, the roadsides became a blaze of colour, with the vast African bush veld as a backdrop and glorious views of the Indian Ocean on our left. When I mentioned earlier that there were no apparent speed limits on the highways, I wasn't prepared for the actual pace at which other vehicles seemed to be driving. Mercedes and BMWs were flying past us at 180 km plus. Christina thought 160 km/h was fast enough.

As we pushed south past the coastal sugarcane town of Amanzimtoti, the surrounding terrain became more rugged, and the highway traversed a more mountainous region. While we took in the spectacular views along one long, sweeping bend, I suddenly had to swerve violently to avoid a large boulder sitting in the middle of the road. It was over a meter high and would have required two men to move it. The rock had obviously been pushed out onto the road. Christina screamed out initially, then held her breath as I wrestled to try and keep control of the Megane, but the car handled brilliantly in the situation. It was one of those OMG, heart-in-the-mouth moments. Immediately after the incident, I thought about stopping, going back and putting a warning sign on the roadside before some other poor soul hit the rock. But whoever pushed the rock out would probably also be watching. It was not a good idea to stop in these parts. Getting out of the car could have been really dangerous.

Earlier in the day, Christina had pointed out a couple of wrecked cars and a bus that had rolled on its side just off the road. We could see people living in the wrecked vehicles, so we thought it would be wiser to push on. We had had a close call, so I slowed to 120 km/h after that incident. The N2 gradually turned west and headed inland around Port Shepstone, where more mountainous ranges loomed ahead of us.

THE ULTRA STATION

It was around mid-afternoon and close to 4 pm. We had travelled nearly 400 kilometres south since leaving Durban that morning, so it was time to think about looking for somewhere to camp for the night. A town called Mthatha (pronounced Um'tata) wasn't far ahead of us. There was a sign for fuel, so we turned off the highway and pulled up at a large walled enclosure with what looked like huge automatic gates and security guards at the entrance. The road led into a service station with a sprawling compound behind. There was an area for caravans, followed by a motel, a swimming pool, and a mini-mart at the back. This was obviously an Ultra Station.

As Mthatha was just a kilometre or two further down the main road, Christina still wanted to go into town to see what the local accommodation had to offer. We turned around and drove out of the Ultra Station and headed into Mthatha, a large central town with impressive colonial-style municipal buildings. We cruised down the main street, spotted a vacant hotel sign and stopped to have a look. When we opened the door and walked up to the reception, the guy behind the desk slowly looked up from his paper and gave us a curious look. The accommodation on offer was like three stars and much cheaper than the Ultra Station. There were several other guests in the place, all black people. Some of them gave us a bit of an odd look as they passed; I had that overwhelming feeling that we did not belong there. Strangers in a strange land, we would be alone, the only white guests in the B&B. Even though the all-black staff were more than friendly, it still felt quite intimidating. Jill's words of warning were ringing in my ears. I told Christina, "Come on, we tried. Let's get back to the Ultra Station before they close, pay the difference, and we can sleep easy." She agreed immediately.

Our night at the Ultra Station was first class. Having a place where we could safely wander around at night for a change felt quite unusual. As we drove away the next morning after breakfast, Christina and I talked about the reality of the situation. We both came to the same conclusion: real integration between black and white people in South Africa was still somewhere way over the horizon. We pushed on. One hundred kilometres further south along the Garden Route, we found ourselves behind a line of vehicles waiting to go through a roadblock. Military vehicles were parked across both lanes. Heavily armed black men in camouflage gear were systematically checking all traffic. Christina didn't like the look of it, but we had no option but to stay in line. When we reached the front of the queue, I was asked to get out of the car. Our ID was checked, then one of the soldiers asked me if I had any weapons. Thankfully we didn't. After checking our car, they let us pass, and we drove on, very relieved but left wondering who or what they were looking for.

The N2 slowly swung west along the Eastern Cape Garden route towards Port Elizabeth, now about 160 km ahead of us. According to our road map, the town of Paterson was around 20 kilometres up a turn-off on the main highway, near the village of Nanga, 60 km before Port Elizabeth. Our original plan was to head straight to the town of Paterson, but a huge storm front was building up in the west just ahead of us. By this time, it was around 3 pm. A towering cumulus cloud with what looked like a gigantic mushroom at the base hovered over the earth, the sky black and ominous below. I said to Christina, "I would crap myself if we were heading into that at sea."

We drove on, and fifteen minutes before we approached the turn-off to Paterson the sky quickly grew dark. The storm was on top of us. Violent thunder and lightning shook the air, followed by hailstones. I had to pull off the road when the visibility dropped to a few meters. The Megane was rocking in the blasts of wind from the storm, I was holding my hands against the back of the windscreen when hail started smashing down on us. We were not the only ones to stop. No one was trying to drive through that maelstrom. While sitting in the car at the side of the road, Christina said, "When this eases up, let's just drive straight into Port Elizabeth tonight. We can start fresh tomorrow and check out the town of Paterson later in the day or on the way back." It sounded like a good plan to me.

We had nothing booked, but Port Elizabeth was a major centre and a popular holiday destination, nestled as it was behind Nelson Mandela Bay on the south coast. Finding safe accommodation there for the night shouldn't be too hard.

PORT ELIZABETH

The hailstones eventually gave way to continuous heavy rain as we drove past the turnoff to Paterson at Nanaga. We reached Port Elizabeth about an hour later, around 6 pm, with the rain still pouring down. It was getting dark. I was peering through the downpour, concentrating on the road ahead, when Christina spotted a hotel with a vacant sign. "Any port in a storm!" I agreed. We pulled off the road, and 10 minutes later we were booked in for the night. A hot meal and a warm bed at the end of another long day.

THE OBELISK

The new day brought a calm, sunny morning after the storm. I went down for breakfast. Christina wasn't that hungry and decided to have a lie in. She asked me if I could get her coffee. As I made my way into the dining room, I caught a stunning view over Nelson Mandela Bay. After my meal, I returned with the coffee. "Christina, you must look at the view from the dining room. I don't know how, but you picked a great spot for us to spend the night." I started packing our luggage while she went for a look.

When Christina entered the dining room, the maître d came over and asked if she would like something to eat or drink, and the purpose of her visit to Port Elizabeth. In reply, Christina explained that it was both a holiday and a curiosity regarding her husband's family name and the town of Paterson. When she mentioned the name John Jack Paterson, he became very animated and exclaimed that John J Paterson was an extremely famous person in the history of Port Elizabeth. He then went on to explain to her some of Paterson's history and his importance to the town as its founding father. After hearing all this, Christina excitedly rushed back to our room and said, "JJ, you're not going to believe this. You have to come and listen to this incredible story." When we returned to the dining room, the maître d introduced himself to me and said, "Oh, I think this would also be of interest to you both," Walking across the room to the window he pointed to a 12-meter-high granite obelisk on a plinth across the road in front of the hotel. He told us that in 1865 John J Paterson erected the obelisk in honour of his great friend and lifelong business partner, George Kemp.

THE HERALD

"Incredible!" I thought. We hadn't even planned to come straight to Port Elizabeth. Nothing was booked, yet somehow Christina had picked this hotel in the middle of that horrendous storm. What were the odds? The maître d said, "I have another idea. Do you mind if I ring a friend? He's a journalist who works for The Herald, our local paper. " Well, what could we say? "OK, sure, let's see where this is all going." Twenty minutes later we were introduced to Ivor Markham. He was not the journalist we expected, but a photographer for the local Port Elizabeth Herald newspaper. After we were introduced, he suggested that we all return to his office to discuss the idea of a story and some pictures that could be published…if we were open to the idea. Fine by me. While we were driving down to Ivor's office in the CBD, I thought, 'Uncle Bill is going to love this little tale.'

After arriving at Ivor's office in the newspaper house we were introduced to Johnnic, a journalist and publisher of the Herald. Johnnic explained that John J Paterson was the founder and original editor of the Eastern Province Herald. He told us they were planning a new masthead for the Herald and said, "You guys have just given me an idea." His proposal, if we were willing to become part of the story, was that he would like to get a photo of me holding the new front-page format for The Herald next to Christina, who would be holding the original very first edition of The Eastern Province Herald dated Wednesday, May 7th, 1845. Cost - one penny! That sounded awesome. Of course, we both wanted to be part of this story. The photo shoot only took 20 minutes. Ivor said if we could wait for half an hour, he would run off a sample copy of the front page just for us. While we were waiting, I told the journalist what little I knew of my Scottish origins.

WE MADE THE HEADLINES

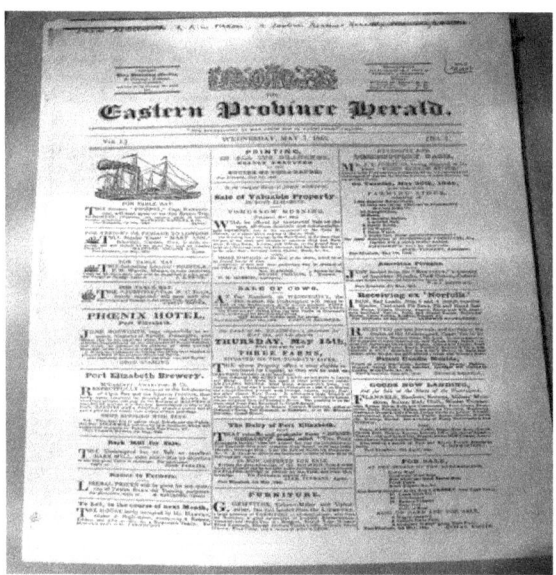
1845 FIRST EDITION

Once that was over, he thanked us and said, "Look, I can see you're both really interested. Would you like to meet our librarian and local historian, Margaret Harradine? She runs the Port Elizabeth City Library and can tell you all there is to know regarding your ancestor. I'll give her a call."

ONE TITAN AT A TIME

The Port Elizabeth City Library is a magnificent, ornate, three-story heritage building with a statue of Queen Victoria in front. It was only a few blocks away from the newspaper house. When we arrived, Margaret, the librarian, greeted us at the door. A warm, friendly lady in her 40s, she was about to take us on a fascinating journey back in time. "Hello, so, your John J Paterson spelt with one 't.' That makes a difference, as there are several different ways to spell your surname. The spelling can relate to different areas and clans in Scotland."

Margaret excused herself and returned shortly with a book entitled ONE TITAN AT A TIME, written about the life and times of John J Paterson by Pamela Folliott in 1960. Margaret invited us into her office. Over a cup of tea, she informed us that he had a nickname, 'Jock', and his family had originated from Aberdeen sometime in the 17th century. I knew nothing of our family history before the 19th century. Margaret went on to tell us that John J Paterson was born in 1822. John was a twin with his sister Jessie. But John was no ordinary twin. His mother, Barbara, was all a flutter because the boy was born with a caul (a membrane that can cover the head and face of a newborn). This was something of great significance to the very superstitious Scots of the day. The caul would be placed in a box that John would always carry...a superstition that would ultimately prove fatal. He was a gifted student who won a scholarship to the University of Aberdeen at the tender age of 14. Six years later, after graduating with honours at 20, he became a schoolteacher. However, John was looking for adventure and decided to become a colonist within the year.

In 1841, at 21 years of age, he migrated to South Africa, specifically to the port of Algoa Bay (known now as Nelson Mandela Bay), a remote outpost on the South African coast. In those early days of the colony, there was no formal education or public schooling. John J Paterson was the very first schoolteacher in Algoa Bay. His teaching position meant he was not supposed to involve himself in local politics or the media. But he was apparently a very vocal individual, so when he became involved in the publication of the first Eastern Cape Herald with a friend, he remained in the background. However, his assertive character eventually broke free, leading him to establish not only the Eastern Province Herald newspaper but also, in 1862, after uniting several influential businessmen, The Standard Bank of South Africa (still the largest bank in South Africa to the present day). He became a prominent member of the South African parliament and a great friend of a young Cecil Rhodes. Together, they pushed the Eastern Cape railway hundreds of kilometres through what is now known as The Garden Route. The town of Paterson is on this line. John also founded the now-revered Grey Boys College in Port Elizabeth.

As his prominence grew, he made several ocean voyages back to London to push his case for the emerging South African colony in the British Parliament. On one of his UK visits, John Paterson was offered a seat at Westminster, which he subsequently turned down. His heart was back in the colony, where he was rumoured to become the next prime minister of South Africa.

At that point in the story, Christina asked Margaret, "Where was he buried? Would it be possible to have a look at his grave?" Margaret's answer caught Christina's breath and sent a shiver down her spine when she said, "Oh no, unfortunately, he was lost at sea on a voyage back to Cape Town from England." I shook my head in disbelief - another John J Paterson lost at sea!

The book ONE TITAN AT A TIME also contained several illustrated pages. On one of them, the obelisk, which we saw earlier in front of our hotel, was depicted as being erected in the centre of town. Margaret flipped to the story of John Paterson's loss at sea towards the end of the book. When she finished the story, I asked her about the town of Paterson. "Yes, it is named in honour of his achievements on the Eastern Cape Rail line, which, as you now know, he jointly constructed with Cecil Rhodes."

Margaret then ran off a copy of some of the most relevant pages from the book for me and wished us both a safe journey. We thanked her again for the fascinating window into history she had revealed for us and stepped back out into the sunshine. What an incredible story…information overload! At the same time, I thought it amazing that no one in my family was aware of this important connection to South Africa's political history. I now have a copy of the book ONE TITAN AT A TIME. A family friend we visited in the UK gave me the book after locating a copy for me on Amazon in 2006.

I have extensively researched the highly unusual circumstances surrounding John J Paterson's demise, and I have taken parts of the following story directly from the book, which is dedicated to his life's work.

THE CAUL

The SS American was not the initial vessel in which John Paterson intended to return to South Africa. I found records that showed that he was due to arrive back in Cape

Town on April 20th aboard the SS German. It seems Paterson had fully intended to sail on that ship, but a friend later received a letter from him in which he mentioned that he was planning to leave England shortly on the SS German. At the beginning of this story, it was established that John J Paterson had been born with a caul. As mentioned earlier, the caul was precious to the superstitious Scot. Possessing a caul guaranteed the owner would never be drowned and apparently granted the owner the gift of second sight. The failure of Paterson to board the SS German had a great bearing on the final events of his life. To get some understanding of the mentality at that time, we can observe the following from the book, ONE TITAN AT A TIME. On page 188, an advertisement for a caul in the 'London Medical Advisor', dated August 1838, reads:

"To be sold for 30 guineas. A child's caul, that has already made 72 voyages in which 38 hurricanes were encountered, besides sundry small storms, without a single drowning taking place. Application to be made to Mr Underwood, Fleet Street. London. NB This caul is particularly suitable for steamboats and hot air balloons!" Paterson was a highly intelligent man, but he was also a Scot, so he had always carried the caul with him on his many trips across the sea. There is no doubt in my mind that he had some presentiment about this final voyage, and the cancellation of his passage at the last moment on the SS German was followed by another late change of plan the following week, when he again cancelled his passage at the 11th hour, this time on the Dublin Castle.

On April 21st, when the Dublin Castle safely arrived in Cape Town, The Eastern Cape Herald announced that Paterson's name was on the passenger list and that he would come at once to Port Elizabeth. But the Herald was ahead of events, and Paterson had not arrived. A Mr

Hume, another passenger on the Dublin Castle, brought with him a letter from Paterson written to a friend in Cape Town the day before the Dublin Castle sailed. In the letter, he said that he had cancelled the trip to await the arrival of his daughter-in-law from South Africa. This sounds like a rather lame excuse, considering the fact that he was due back as a major representative for the opening of the Cape Town Parliament. The arrival of his daughter-in-law may or may not have been the real reason. I suspect he could have misplaced his caul when visiting several relatives in Scotland shortly before his departure date, which would have made him very uneasy about his imminent voyage. The Herald later announced that this letter delivered by Mr Hume was the last letter ever written by Paterson, but again, the Herald publishers were wrong!

Paterson then booked a third passage to South Africa on the SS American. Shortly before the SS American was due to depart, I discovered that he had decided to do something totally out of character, hastily writing a new will on just two sheets of paper. Did he create this new will because he had misplaced his caul? We will never know, but these final acts suggest a man under considerable pressure. Was he desperately trying to locate his lost caul? A proud yet superstitious Scot, was he possibly too embarrassed to admit that he hadn't departed from the UK on the first ship, the SS German because he had lost his caul, which would have exposed him to ridicule by his peers in Westminster?

"THE SS AMERICAN HAS FOUNDERED AT SEA."

On April 30th, 1880, The Eastern Cape Herald announced that the SS American would arrive in Cape Town on May 1st. The parliament was due to open on

May 7th, but Paterson's seat was empty. What had happened to the SS American?

The SS American was only 7 years old in 1880 and, at 320 feet long, weighing 2426 tons, was one of the fastest ocean liners of the day, capable of 12 knots. Before departure, Captain A. Maclean hoped to set a new record for the Southampton to Cape Town run, which would have guaranteed the mail contract for the Union Shipping line. The 68 passengers were looking forward to a traditional crossing of the line ceremony later that day, as the SS American was less than 3 degrees north of the equator and heading South. But at 5 am on the 23rd of April, there was an almighty explosion from the engine room. The propeller shaft disintegrated, smashing into the riveted hull and tearing a huge hole below the waterline. The chief engineer managed to stop the engine, but the flood of water was way beyond the pumps, and the captain gave the order to man the lifeboats.

There are various accounts of the catastrophe by a number of the survivors. Still John Paterson wrote this following letter (from onboard the also ill-fated SS Senegal) to his friend Mr Kirkwood and gives the story in the greatest detail. His widow in London found this letter in his luggage, which was forwarded to her after his death It was ironic the box with Paterson's caul was not recorded in the luggage. Paterson was anticipating the arrival of the SS Senegal at Grand Canary Island, which meant that this last letter was written only hours before his death.

The following letter by John J Paterson is recorded in the book, ONE TITAN AT A TIME, pages 190-91.

"My dear Mr Kirkwood, you will have heard by telegram of the sad fate of the American, in which I was a party to the Cape. All went well in her; (despite an alteration in her furnace, we could not get anything of a good run out of her). 5'oclock aroused by a terrible noise and a shaking of the vessel from stem to stern. I hastened on deck to see what the matter was. But at first, I could learn nothing. The engineer had succeeded by this time in stopping the engine, but not before what I suspect was the broken shaft of the vessel had so smashed in a portion of the stern of the vessel or torn to pieces the shaft tube that the water poured in with such force and volume that soon all discovered the vessel to be sinking. No screaming. No unseemly demonstration. Passengers, stunned and in semi- consciousness, did what they were told. They went at 8 o'clock for a little breakfast prepared for them like the last meal. Few partook of it, however. Then, to orders to get ready for the boats, ladies first, they went methodically through the effort, each one taking the smallest bag as containing all that he or she could have beyond the clothes that in which they stood. And then quietly they went into the boats, and I, myself being the last of the passengers to leave. At about 10 o'clock, the chief engineer thought that with the aid of the donkey engine and a good relay of volunteers at the pumps, he could keep the water from gaining further head on us. But although the young men in the boats answered promptly to a call to the pumps, their best efforts were unavailing. The vessel was seen to be sinking fast astern, and before the Captain himself left at about 11 o'clock, the whole poop was underwater, with the sea washing down the companionway. All boats were now ordered away from the vessel's side, except the Captain's boat in which I was, and we kept within some five hundred yards of her until, at last, about 12.05. her stern went down, and she rose by the bow like a great sea monster, rearing back until she bought her masts and funnel down level with the waves. She then plunged down with a tremendous crash and the roar of rushing water, leaving nothing but the wreckage of loose items on her deck, accompanied. by a winding sheet of white foam to mark the spot." (A position only a handful of miles south from where my uncle J J Paterson on the SS Cerinthus would be torpedoed sixty-two years later, in 1942.) The letter continues: "There was a little fleet of eight small boats, 141 souls: no land nearer than Cape Palmas, on the West coast of Africa 220 miles distance. All shaped their course for this point, with instructions to keep together. But they soon separated, and occasionally, we sighted a companion sail. When, on Saturday morning, no sail was in sight, a sense of solitariness was experienced in full. Still, we hoped we did not despair. We trusted; we did not respond. A long and hard Saturday. Nineteen people packed in the boat. The sun was terrific. Daily allowance of one pint of water; the thirst was becoming that burning thirst which is so soon intolerable and ends in delirium. All eyes strained to see some strange sail if possible, and sure enough, even in that unlikely quarter of the sea, where few sails are ever seen, a strange sail, small at first as a man's hand, was described on the horizon. Every now and then, it disappeared behind the waves, but as we headed our little craft towards it, the sail came more and more into view, and a little more than two hours from the time of discovering it. We were alongside an American barque, THE EMMA F. HARRIMAN. (An armed sailing ship of the day). We were received on board by as kind a Captain as ever extended succour to a shipwrecked crew. It appeared that the captain, as soon as he had heard of our sad tale, stopped his vessel for the whole of Saturday night to see if he could pick up any more boats. Then, later, I picked up two additional boats. Sixty-five souls were rescued altogether. The following Monday, a roaring tornado struck us; thunder, lightning, and rain, as it can only in these tropical regions. The captain was all ready for the storm, with no sail up but the lower topsails, and we drove before the blast without damage. About midnight, the steamer Goanza of the British and West African line, in answer to our blue signal lights and firing guns, came alongside, and in less than an hour, we were all transferred to this friendly sail. Which went back with us to a place called Grand Bassam (on the Ivory Coast, West Africa), where the Captain of the Coanza said we would be taken up by the first homeward-bound vessel for England. We remained there kindly treated by the local Liberians, a free negro population, till the next Saturday morning, when we were then taken onboard SS. Senegal, (a French 3200-ton cargo passenger liner) commanded by Captain Kean, which was homeward bound for England. We carried on to Sierra Leone and remained sometime awaiting the movements of the Governor, Sir Samuel Rowe, who was to be a passenger by us. Sir Samuel was one of those rough rollicking gentlemen, who are so often very kind of heart, but who seem to have no other way of showing kindness than by something in the way of jollifications. He and the Captain seemed to have resolved to give to a few of us at the next station where the steamer stopped, namely Bathurst on the Gambia coast, what, if one might introduce the unhallowed word here, be called a "spree." But I myself declined the invitation to it, and at the request of nearly all my companions in disaster, pressed upon Sir Samuel not to delay the vessel for any business which could possibly stand over. The appeal to him of our anxiety to get on to Madeira, that as soon as possible we might by telegram relieve our relations and friends of their anxiety was not very well received. Two inconsiderate unnamed ladies of my party went ashore and accepted the invitation at Bathurst. And danced till early morning . Surely such conduct was not to be commended. Even for appearances sake? We lost 24 hours, and most of the party after exposing themselves to the night air contracted coast fever and thus spread the fever all through the ship. Further I have lost in the wreck everything which I had, not merely all my clothes but that which I stood up in, but all papers and documents as well.

Finally in no case could I be with you before about the middle of June, when the first of these two great measures, in which I took, as indeed the people of Port Elizabeth did. I mean the confederate and the new railway measures. So, under these arduous circumstances I am driven now to resolve to close my political connection with the dear old colony. (No more ocean voyages without his caul?) Not willingly do I do so, yet by a power to which we must all bend, must I now in this matter bend. Enclose to you for Sir David Tennant my resignation of the seat for Port Elizabeth so that if there is time for another representative to be elected, the constituency may suffer as little as possible. Convey you to them the assurance of my customary regard, and add that although now there is, through this terrible ship disaster, a severance forever of our political connection, nothing but the severance of the cord of life itself will separate me in feeling, affection and regard for my many dear friends in Port Elizabeth. Tell them when you return among them (Kirkwood was waiting for Paterson in Cape Town for the opening session of parliament) that to any and every one of them visiting England, my house and my heart will ever be open. To my many friends in parliament, also my warmest expressions of regard. As I think over the fact that I will never again mingle among them, my heart is ready to give way within me. Yet that day had to come when I should no longer be a member of the house. I may never revisit South Africa, but you must and will revisit England. Come then to me and stay with me, and we shall go over our intertwined past with a strangely weird double play of sweetness and sadness. If you choose, you may give this account to my good friend, St. Léger.
Yours affectionately. John J Paterson." *
(Mr St Leger was the editor of the Cape Times).

*Folliott; P.; 1960; ONE TITAN AT A TIME; pages 190 – 191

It would appear from this last letter that Paterson had intended to stay in England permanently and decided not to risk any more sea voyages without his caul. A huge decision, considering his highly successful career in South African politics and the very real possibility that he could have become South Africa's next Prime Minister.

SHIPWRECKED A SECOND TIME

I have constructed this last chapter of John J Paterson's life from the conflicting evidence of other passengers and crew on the SS Senegal. There is also an account by Lloyds Shipping of London. John must have finished his letter shortly before Senegal reached its next port of call.

The Grand Canary Islands are nearly 1300 km north of Bathurst off the coast of West Africa. Captain Kean, the skipper of Senegal, was very experienced in these waters, but when making his final approach at dead slow speed into Melerino Bay, he hit an uncharted rock near Grand Point. The captain immediately decided to run the Senegal aground as they were so close to the shore. The weather was fine, the sea calm. He then planned to send all the passengers the short distance safely ashore in lifeboats, according to one of the passengers who had also been on the SS American. When the order was given to man the lifeboats, panic broke out among the passengers, not unnaturally, as this was the second time in less than a month that some of them had been shipwrecked.

What followed was exactly the reverse behaviour of the orderly conduct experienced when the SS American went down. It was also reported that the crew of the Senegal had apparently not practised any lifeboat drills since leaving their last port either. People took matters into their own hands and scrambled over each other to get into the boats. Despite the panic and confusion, all the lifeboats were successfully lowered except for the last one. Paterson, unlike the other passengers, had not panicked and patiently waited. He and several of the crew boarded the final lifeboat. Then Fate stepped in. When the lifeboat was swung out on the davits, at that very same instant, someone on board Senegal released the bow tackle without permission. The heavy bow tackle boom plunged down and hit the lifeboat midships. The impact cut the lifeboat instantly in two. The occupants all fell into the water alongside the hull. Lifebuoys were immediately thrown over, and a nearby fishing boat picked up all the survivors but one.

The chief engineer witnessed the whole incident from the deck of Senegal and said Mr Paterson was swept along the hull, desperately waving his arms, and then disappeared under the stern near the propeller, never to be seen again. Everyone else on board the SS Senegal was saved with only one loss of life…John J Paterson. He was 58 years old. Was his premonition regarding the loss of his caul before leaving England finally to be proved fatally, correct years later?

To honour Paterson's memory, a paddle steamer was renamed John Paterson in Cape Town, only to also sink in 1906. The SS Senegal was subsequently re-floated and, after major repairs, continued in service. Still, exactly 7 years later, in 1887, she struck rocks at Tabou Point, coincidentally again off the West African coast of Liberia and sank a second time.

I uncovered another weird link. Among the Senegal's passenger list was a young army officer, Athol Paterson, son of the late John J Paterson of Port Elizabeth. All the passengers were saved. But here is another strange twist. Years later, during the First World War, Athol was returning to the UK on leave from South Africa when he was reported missing overboard, and yes, incredibly off the coast of West Africa. John J Paterson's son, another family member, lost at sea in the very same area as his father. Sixty years later, in 1942. The SS Cerinthus, bound for Freetown, also on the Ivory Coast of West Africa, would be torpedoed south of the Cape Verde Islands in the same area of the globe where John J Paterson's days came to an end. My Uncle John J Paterson also survived the initial sinking of the SS Cerinthus, only to similarly perish at a later date. Hard to believe so many strange twists of fate with the same family name and in the same area of the sea.

THE TOWN OF PATERSON

By the time Christina and I left the Port Elizabeth library, it was mid-afternoon, so after a quick bite to eat, we decided to head out of Port Elizabeth, back to the N2 and make for our original destination, Paterson, 70 km inland from Port Elizabeth. We didn't it know then, but the guys at The Herald had already rung ahead of us to let them know we were on our way. It was a 40-minute drive. We turned off the main road at the Nanaga intersection. Christina spotted a sign for the Addo Elephant Reserve. We drove for a while alongside the biggest electric fence I have ever seen, around 4 meters high. (It looked like the dinosaur fence in Jurassic Park!) I wondered what kind of voltage would be needed to keep elephants enclosed.

Once past the elephant park, the road sign for the town of Paterson came into view, just a railway siding built on the Eastern Cape rail line running east-west. As we approached from the South, our first impression of the town was a real shock, not what we expected. On both sides of the road leading up to the rail line running through the town was a huge slum. Hundreds of people were living in extreme poverty under sheets of tin and rags stretched over poles, power cords like spaghetti running in all directions.

We slowed down, drove past and then over the rail line into the main street of a pristine little village. We were greeted with white picket fences, manicured lawns and rose gardens. Passing by local shops, we eventually pulled up outside the small, whitewashed Paterson Hotel. We grabbed our bags and made our way to the reception. After identifying ourselves, we were in for an unexpected surprise. The phrase 'being treated like royalty' is the simplest way to describe what happened next. A welcome committee awaited us, and I was presented with the hotel register to sign a historic John J Paterson sign-in.

The locals made a grand occasion of our arrival. Christina thought all the attention was completely over the top when the owner of the Paterson Hotel hosted a lovely meal for us, with a couple of town council members and their wives present. It was a truly unforgettable evening. Everyone wanted to know all about us, asking endless questions regarding the Australian way of life. As the meal ended, we were invited to a tour of the tiny town the following morning. What a memorable day, finishing with the town's generous hospitality and a great overnight stay.

The following morning, after breakfast, we were introduced to the town clerk and taken for a tour of Paterson. There is not a lot to see at a railway siding with a population of only around 800. The African community on the other side of the rail tracks didn't get a mention, but while we were being shown around town, a couple of men from the slum gingerly approached our party. One of them asked our town official if they could get permission to bury their dead in the white cemetery, as their black graveyard was at capacity. We were informed that the aids virus was decimating them. There didn't seem to be any government care or medical help for these people. I think our hosts were a bit embarrassed by the request, but they told the representatives from the camp that they would have to make other arrangements, as only whites are allowed to be buried in their cemetery. Christina and I thought they were a bit heartless and had turned a blind eye to the other side of the rail line, pretending those poor souls in the camp just didn't exist.

To be fair to the residents of Paterson, South Africa was run by an all-black majority government at the time, the ANC. So, the health and well-being of the black community across the tracks were not the townspeople of Paterson's personal responsibility. Still, that incident took some of the shine off an otherwise very enjoyable stay.

As we prepared to leave, Christina reflected on how this truly felt like a 'once-in-a-lifetime' adventure. Saying our goodbyes to our wonderful hosts and driving out of Paterson through the slum camp left me feeling a bit flat. I thought this was it. We had reached the end of our journey, and there didn't seem to be anything else to discover about the story of Paterson. But what an incredible story. It had been the road trip of a lifetime, filled with memories, and we had discovered another John J Paterson lost at sea.

LESOTHO

It was time to plan the return journey home to Empangeni, but Christina was still curious. She had heard about a country called Lesotho and wanted to take a detour. Inland, about 300 km to the north and nestled inside the Drakensberg Mountain Range, Lesotho was a tiny self-governing and independent country with a border of only nine hundred kilometres entirely encircled by South Africa. It was a big detour, but it did sound interesting. After leaving Paterson, we backtracked about 150 kilometres along the Eastern Cape Road, then north before turning inland towards the Drakensberg mountains. The main highway gave way to a 'B' road, which degraded into an unsealed surface as the spectacular Drakensberg Mountain range grew before us like a mile-high wall of ragged monolithic rock, locally referred to as the Dragon's teeth. Our little Megane was not happy bouncing along in those harsh conditions. We followed the signs into a ravine between the mountains that eventually opened out at a border post, a small Customs building next to a huge sign declaring 'Lesotho, the highest country in the world'.

No part of Lesotho is below 1200 meters above sea level, and the highest peaks are around 4000 meters. We drove up to the barrier, and the Customs Officer approached our car and asked to see our passports. That was the moment when we both felt stupid. Before we left Empangeni, the possibility that we might get robbed seemed very real, and a British passport was worth gold on the black market. At the same time, if we were robbed of our passports, we would have been left stranded in South Africa, so we decided to leave our passports at Bill's place. I didn't think there would be any need for them while travelling internally around South Africa.

The customs guy could see our predicament and smiled. He was very understanding, but we could not enter Lesotho without a passport. And that was as close as we got to the tiny kingdom of Lesotho. We turned the Megane around and backtracked down the dusty road out of the mountains, just managing to reach a safe hotel which was recommended in the tourist guide before sundown.

After breakfast, another day-long scenic drive through the African bushveld, and we were back in Empangeni for a late evening meal at Bill's place. Mission accomplished. We both felt the tension slip away, that safe, secure, good-to-be-home feeling after a crazy week on the road.

PORT RICHARDS

We still had a few days of our holiday left, so Bill suggested that we take a look at Port Richards, his previous place of employment as assistant Harbour Master, before retiring. The drive to the port only took 10 minutes, and Bill introduced us to the current Harbourmaster and his former boss. I wish I could recall his name, but I do remember his car, a truly impressive black V12 Mercedes Pullman 600. Christina and I were treated to a luxurious personal tour around the biggest coal loading terminal in the world built in a vast natural bay that is also the estuarine entrance to the Mizingazi wetlands river system of lakes. While we were cruising around the terminal, the conversation turned to sailing, so our host invited us over to the very upmarket Zululand Yacht Club for lunch, where he was a member. It was recently built on the banks of a thirty-meter-wide river mouth that spills into a beautiful corner of the bay, surrounded by a couple of small islands. The banks were lined with mansions along with big power boats moored up next to personal jetties, in stark contrast to the massive coal terminal on the other side of the bay.

We had a great lunch together at the marina, and during the meal, I became involved in a long conversation with the harbourmaster. He told me that occasionally he was requested by the World Health Organisation and other major charitable NGOs to travel along the coast with his crew to supervise the unloading of aid ships carrying emergency equipment. Food supplies, tractors, pumps, tents, whatever. Then he asked me to guess the percentage of those goods that would reach the people they were intended for. I thought for a second and said, "I don't know, maybe 40%. He smiled and shook his head. "That would be nice, but the sad truth is, only around 3% of all the aid and charitable goods coming into South Africa at the moment will reach those people in the original fashion intended". Next, he described what happened on a recent assignment to supervise the unloading of medical equipment from a mercy ship hundreds of kilometres north along the coast of Mozambique.

THE HARBOUR MASTER'S STORY

Shortly after arriving to start work with his team, a truckload of heavily armed men drove onto the wharf and ordered them all back into their vehicles at gunpoint. Then, they could only sit and watch for hours as the entire medical cargo was stolen and transferred on to another ship. The armed men disappeared after the ship had sailed with the stolen goods. That's the way it goes. Everything ends up on the black market or in the hands of a local village chief. I asked, "Surely the police or local government can provide security in that sort of circumstance?" He said, "Yes, of course, we always contact the authorities ahead of time, but repeatedly, we experience the military conveniently showing up when all the bad guys are gone." Everybody gets a slice of the cake. Sadly, the corruption in South Africa seemed to be endemic at all levels.

After lunch, Christina and I took a stroll around the newly constructed Zulu marina. We walked to the end of one of the jetties. Gazing out about 100 metres into the bay, I couldn't help but smile when I noticed a sign protruding from the water. Beware of hippos! The sign depicted the head of a yawning hippo. Then, while making our way back along the jetty, I spotted a group of around twenty hippos in the water right by the bank near the clubhouse. I wondered whether the Zulu Yacht Club was the only one in the world with such a unique sign warning yachties about hippos. I asked a guy who was working in the hardstand area if crocodiles or hippos had ever come up the launching ramp. "Oh, not now, but they used to be really bad before all the development. You still have to be aware. Definitely no swimming!"

GOING HOME

With only one day left before the long drive back to Johannesburg, Bill invited a few friends over that night for a drink and one last get together. A couple we were talking to thought our road trip down to Paterson was reckless. "Don't you read the papers? You drove all that way without a gun? So many desperate people wandering around... crazy!" Another friend of Bill's wanted to know all about moving to Australia after nearly 50% of his farm had been repossessed by the ANC. He told me that he was at his wit's end. New ANC government legislation now meant he could only employ his children in the family business. Any other employee must be an indigenous African person.

We soon learned that there were literally thousands of white people and their families who wanted to get out of the South. Africa. 'Packing for Perth' was a popular phrase we had heard mentioned many times. Then my cousin Jill turned on the TV and said, "Hey, has anyone seen Big Brother? It's a new show. You wouldn't believe it! They have a black guy in the house, living with white people!" Everyone in the room crowded around the telly in disbelief. Christina looked across at me. I stood back. We didn't want to make a comment. Why would a black guy in the Big Brother house be such a big issue? The program had already aired on Australian TV the year before. This reaction to the TV show really highlighted the enormous cultural divide and simmering tensions between the black and the now very much in the minority white population. (Eight months later Uncle Bill and Jill survived a violent home invasion. They then decided enough was enough, sold up and returned safely back to Scotland to join the rest of the family near Edinburgh).

On our last morning in Empangeni, we had a family breakfast together and said our final goodbyes to my Uncle Bill (not easy when you know it's the last time.) Another extended drive inland brought us to Johannesburg. Jill dropped us at the airport. After one last big hug, I said, "Take care of Bill and thank you for everything." An hour or so later, there were sighs of relief from both of us when we boarded the plane and finally fastened our seat belts. We had made it, and were still in one piece.

As we prepared for take-off, I sank back into my seat and all the events of the last month started flooding through my head. The Thangami hot springs adventure and the amazing coincidence we stumbled upon at Port Elizabeth with John J. Paterson, also lost at sea. Ending up on the front page of the Port Elizabeth Herald, with historic family connections to the founder. Quite a ride! As we were taking off, I said to Christina, "All this stuff about whites bringing AIDS into South Africa gives you a guilty feeling just for being white." So many native African people were dying from the AIDS HIV virus, and we were having to deal with the terrible misinformation that was on TV, radio, and the press. Oddly, I think we experienced first-hand how it feels to be part of an oppressed minority group: intimidating and more than just a bit scary.

We talked about South Africa's long-term future on the flight home. Nelson Mandela had been released from his Robben Island prison after 27 years in 1993. A year later, after the first democratic general elections were held, the all-black majority ANC came into power. Everyone thought there would be a new dawn of a golden age for

South Africa, but corruption and greed seemed to have undermined every corner of the country, and the promised healthcare system appeared to be non-existent. White people in business were looking at a bleak future, living in fear for their lives. Christina thought it was so sad that such a beautiful country, with everything seemingly going for it, was slowly slipping into chaos and anarchy.

At a farewell gathering shortly before Christina and I left Australia, friends shared the programme of their upcoming African safari. They would fly into S.A. and spend their first night at a top hotel in Johannesburg, then a helicopter flight out to one of the big game parks the next day. Ten days in a 5-star lodge, no problems, all catered for, a great time with everybody nice and friendly. Then, after their safari was over, fly safely back to Australia. On the other hand, Christina and I had personally experienced the journey of a lifetime in the real South Africa at ground level…the one that tourists will never see and we will never forget.

Months after our return to Australia, I sought a direct family link to John J Paterson of Port Elizabeth, South Africa. This was not an easy task, given that the same surname appears throughout Scottish historical records. For me, there exists the sense of another connection. Merely being directly related doesn't alter the facts. My uncle Jack's life ended in a similar manner to that of John J Paterson of Port Elizabeth, and both men met their fate in the same part of the ocean, off the coast of West Africa. Both survived the initial sinking, only to perish at a later date. I suppose I was the lucky one. (They didn't have an EPIRB!) Did the rescue make a difference in my life? Absolutely! Now, when I hear some of my friends worrying about the future and how much time is left, I think back to another place and time when all that mattered was the next wave.

Fatalistic is not how I would have previously described myself. "God doesn't play dice with the universe," Einstein once famously said. So, for the logical thinker, there is always a rational explanation. But when it all gets crazy, when bizarre outcomes and life seem to spiral out of control, we tend to revert to "It's just a coincidence, a twist of fate." Totally illogical! So, has fate played a hand here? It's too hard for me to figure it out. What I do know is that I have had a lot of fun digging through time and putting this story together. In some way, the three individual stories of our lives have become intertwined over the centuries, linking us all in this extraordinary tale of our coincidental history.

JOHN AND CHRISTINA PATERSON

And…we're still cruising!

END

ACKNOWLEDGEMENTS

As a first-time author I believed I had the bones of a good story, but had no idea what it takes to turn an idea into a book. Without the assistance of the following people, I'm sure it would have all been too hard. During a chance meeting with Howard Moses, an old sailing buddy of mine, I mentioned that I was considering writing my story and he offered to help. He had previously worked with the Fremantle Television Institute and the ABC in Darwin, producing several short documentaries. That initial connection was serendipitous, as Howard was also the first friend I caught up with after our repatriation from the Cocos Islands in 1992. He clearly remembered how fired up I was on the day I downloaded the whole story to him. Howard also introduced me to Chris Bowman, a self-published author who has patiently guided me through the publication process and also designed the book's cover. When I needed help transforming my initial draft into something resembling a book, my good friend De-Anne Cole came to my rescue, navigating me through the complexities of Word and computer-speak. Before publication, all books need a professional edit, and again, a friend and academic, Rhonda James, did a first-class job. Last but certainly not least, my darling Christina, for her unending patience. To you all I give my most heartfelt thanks.

www.ingramcontent.com/pod-product-compliance
Lightning Source LLC
Chambersburg PA
CBHW062033290426
44109CB00026B/2612